P9-AQD-893

Business Etiquette

101 Ways to Conduct Business with Charm and Savvy

By
Ann Marie Sabath

CAREER PRESS
3 Tice Road
P.O. Box 687
Franklin Lakes, NJ 07417
1-800-CAREER-1
201-848-0310 (NJ and outside U.S.)
FAX: 201-848-1727

Copyright © 1998 by Ann Marie Sabath

All rights reserved under the Pan-American and International Copyright Conventions. This book may not be reproduced, in whole or in part, in any form or by any means electronic or mechanical, including photocopying, recording, or by any information storage and retrieval system now known or hereafter invented, without written permission from the publisher, The Career Press.

BUSINESS ETIQUETTE
Cover design by Hub Graphics Corp.
Printed in the U.S.A. by Book-mart Press

To order this title, please call toll-free 1-800-CAREER-1 (NJ and Canada: 201-848-0310) to order using VISA or Master Card, or for further information on books from Career Press.

Library of Congress Cataloging-in-Publication Data

Sabath, Ann Marie.
    Business etiquette : 101 ways to conduct business with charm and savvy / by Ann Marie Sabath.
        p.   cm.
    Includes index.
    ISBN 1-56414-322-8 (pbk.)
    1. Business etiquette.   I. Title.
HF5389.S228   1998
395.5'2--dc21

97-35239
CIP

Praise for
Business Etiquette

"This book teaches individuals how to represent their companies, their products, and themselves with confidence, polish, warmth, and professionalism."

—*John Daw, Vice President of Field Sales, Marriott Lodging*

"Gets right to the heart of the matter. An invaluable resource for anyone whose work involves interaction with others—and that's just about all of us."

—*Brandon Toropov, author,* The Complete Idiot's Guide to Getting Along with Difficult People

"Helps individuals to determine which behaviors to maintain and which to modify in order to achieve confidence and, ultimately, success in the world of business."

—*Robyn M. Hildal, Ed. D., Human Resources Manager, The E.W. Scripps Company*

"Up-to-date and easy to read—a big departure from most business etiquette books."

—*Sheila Casserly, President, Celebrity Focus*

"Assists individuals in enhancing their understanding of the 'perception impact.'"

—*William H. Bagley,*
Human Resources Professional

"Both young and old, experienced and novice alike can benefit from this book."

—*C. Dean Ferguson, Director of*
Educational Services, Delta Sigma Pi

Acknowledgments

My acknowledgments go to...

That man of vision, my publisher, Ron Fry.

My parents, Mary and Camille Sabath, whose actions taught me both the work ethic and the importance of hospitality.

My Aunt Nell who showed me that "What you do is important, however, the way you do it is even more important."

My children, Scott and Amber, who have been my "test cases" for grooming the "McManners" Generation.

My dearest Thomas Byron who continues to be my sounding board regarding what is "appropriate."

My colleague, Suzy, whose attention to detail exemplifies the way all organizations should conduct business.

Elin Woodger, who helped with text development and editing.

My literary agent, Brandon Toropov, who made this book a reality.

Our client companies who have requested us to reinforce to their teams the importance of doing business with charm and savvy.

My *Cincinnati Downtowner* newspaper readers who have submitted questions about their own business courtesy dilemmas.

Our many business etiquette hotline callers who allow us to assist them in overcoming their "moments of hesitation."

Our certification graduates who assist our organization in preparing present and future business leaders to live by "The Golden Rule."

Contents

Why You Need This Book

Let's face it—proper behavior in business settings can be a scary topic. Being unsure of what move should come next in a work-related situation is often quite unnerving. When we're scared, we don't think very well. That can make successful interaction with professional contacts seem almost impossible.

Like most of us, you've no doubt asked yourself plenty of questions about conduct in the workplace, questions that don't seem to have easy answers:

- "What, exactly, am I supposed to wear on dress-down day?"

- "How do I handle people who come across too strong during meetings?"

- "What's the best way to compose an e-mail message to my most important prospective client?"

- "When I'm conducting business in a foreign country, what should I say—or avoid saying—to my host?"

These are the kinds of questions that can keep people up at night. I know, because I work every day with people who've lost sleep over matters of business behavior—people who are eager, as you are, to learn how to conduct business with charm and savvy. Through my business, At Ease, Inc., I provide business protocol services and training through live seminars, videos, print media, and a telephone hotline service. I've trained thousands of individuals and have worked with such organizations as Fidelity Investments, Procter & Gamble, Cap Gemini America, United Brands, the Huffy Corporation, Showtime Network, Inc., Saks Fifth Avenue, SmithKline Beecham, BP America, Paychex, MCI Telecommunications, the Marriott Corporation, and Salomon Brothers. I've also worked with countless small businesses in addressing the same etiquette and protocol questions that trouble representatives of the bigger companies.

How did I get started in my business? After graduating from college and doing some experimenting in the work world, I began to watch what people were doing to get ahead in their organizations. I realized that the ones who knew how to make the best impression and how to make others feel comfortable in social situations were the ones who often got a leg up on the competition. So about 10 years ago, I started taking some notes and eventually started a new company. My aim was to help companies get the "sand" out of their employees' social "gears" and, as a result, to increase their bottom lines.

Guess what? It worked!

Who is this book for?

Business Etiquette: 101 Ways to Conduct Business with Charm and Savvy is for you—whether you've just landed an entry-level office job, operate on the front lines with people who use your company's product or service, run your own business, or hold any other position that involves maintaining business relationships with others. Whether you work for a multinational corporation, a local print shop, or a one-person business, you have probably faced the same basic question my clients have: How do I make sure I don't say or do the wrong thing in a business setting?

Often, I am challenged by seminar participants to provide a single, one-sentence answer to that question, an answer that applies to any and all business situations. You may be surprised to learn that such an answer actually exists!

The guiding principle

This book is full of practical advice that will help you come across with charm and savvy in a wide variety of business settings. Before you take advantage of this targeted counsel, however, you may be interested in learning more about the underlying principle that I believe is always—repeat, *always*—there for you to fall back on in business situations. Here's my one-sentence answer to that question my clients always ask:

Make the individual with whom you're dealing feel as though he or she were the most important person in the world.

When you come right down to it, that's the secret to managing business protocol and etiquette issues. Naturally, there's a lot more advice to bear in mind. But all of it, I believe, relies on making the other person feel important, attended to, respected. It's a natural human tendency: We like to spend time with—and will often go out of our way to help—people who make us feel like a million bucks.

This guiding principle is simple, memorable, and—surprise, surprise—capable of imparting just about everyone with a new sense of confidence in approaching even complex issues of etiquette and protocol in the workplace.

Conducting business with charm and savvy means making an investment of attention in the other person, nothing more and nothing less. That principle applies whether you're picking up an important executive at the airport, or whether you're explaining an unfamiliar office policy to a wayward subordinate.

Conducting business with charm and savvy means making an effort to learn more about others than you share about yourself. It means learning to interact with others more effectively by consistently putting a positive focus on the person on the other side. It means being present for the individual with whom you're interacting and making sure he or she feels great about the exchange.

Interest in and concern for others supports all "proper etiquette." In my own experience, undivided attention may be the single best technique for banishing that queasy "what do I do now" feeling many of us associate with social encounters related to our work.

The specific applications presented in this book—all 101 of them—reinforce the basic principle in ways you can easily use. When you *know* you're doing the right thing and recognize how to do it, you feel more confident, better informed, and better prepared for the challenges that come your way during the workday.

So much for the etiquette jitters!

A simple, no-nonsense guide

Part of what makes business etiquette and protocol seem so intimidating at first glance is the apparent complexity of "proper conduct." Many etiquette books, business-related and otherwise, resemble fat dictionaries or legal resources, with column upon column of dense type. These books often leave readers reeling with the question, "How am I ever going to remember all that?"

Business Etiquette isn't one of those guides. It won't spend page after page outlining intricate, hard-to-remember theories and systems for you to follow. But it *will* offer concrete advice that will help you in specific situations.

The aim of this book is to assist you in conducting your business with more confidence, know-how, grace, and efficiency than ever before. I've written this book on the principle that little things really do mean a lot. Little things are, after all, what make other people feel special. Accordingly, this book will outline plenty of "little steps" you can take—steps that, one by one, will help you:

- Put others at ease by showing more confidence and poise in business settings.

- Handle moments of hesitation with a style that leaves your contacts feeling glad you were there.

- Negotiate more "win-win" outcomes.

In short, this book will help you master the neglected art of making people feel good about themselves!

How this book is arranged

This book is divided into specific areas of business, each offering practical solutions that are critical to your success.

For example, Chapter 1 shows you how to handle initial contact. If you've ever wondered how to manage greetings and introductions, what to do when a name escapes you, or when to pass along a business card, you'll want to take a look at the advice here.

Chapter 2 gives you all the advice you need on attire issues in the workplace: What exactly is "business casual"? What do you do if your company hasn't set down clear guidelines about what's acceptable attire and what isn't? How should you handle subordinates whose dress is clearly unprofessional?

Whether you're interested in making your business correspondence look as sharp as it possibly can, using fax messages to make a positive impression, or sending e-mail that gets noticed for all the right reasons, you'll find plenty of helpful suggestions in Chapter 3.

Lapses in business etiquette over the telephone are usually among the most dangerous (and neglected) enemies of any organization's bottom line. Chapter 4 shows you ways to use this common business communication tool to your best advantage.

Chapter 5 is where you'll find the Twelve Commandments of Cubicle Etiquette and more great advice on harmonious interaction with the people sharing your workplace.

In Chapter 6 you'll learn how to make the most of meetings and how to clear all the common hurdles—without ruffling the feathers of subordinates, peers, or supervisors.

If you've ever felt flustered when dealing with a CEO or other potentially prickly "top dog," you'll want to study Chapter 7, offering the lowdown on handling people in high places.

Poise and confidence may count for even more when you're away from the office on business. Chapter 8 shows you how to display charm and savvy at parties, receptions, restaurants—any time you're away from your "home turf."

Personal crises? Prescription medication? Job offers? The way you address these and similar challenges can lead to catastrophe if you're not careful. Chapter 9 offers the best ways to handle some relatively uncommon, but potentially serious, questions of protocol and behavior.

The final chapter features some common questions and interesting business etiquette problems that readers of my newspaper column have brought to my attention—and the solutions I recommend. See how the real-world challenges of my readers compare with your own.

In addition to the 101 etiquette tips focusing on business close to home, you'll also find a helpful appendix that outlines the essentials of *international* etiquette. Whether you're planning on doing business in Australia, Japan, the United Kingdom, or the other countries covered, you can prepare for your encounters with this review of the do's and don'ts of conducting business throughout the world.

Where to begin?

How should you read this book? There are two ways to go: One is simply to start from the first tip and work your way through to the end. This will give you the opportunity to conduct a thorough review of, and gain an in-depth understanding of my approach to, the various issues covered. The other way to read this book is to consult it as the need arises—scan the contents and find the chapter heading that applies to the situation you now face. Either technique, or a combination of the two, is acceptable. There is no "wrong" way to track down the information you need. This book has been arranged for ease of use and fast access.

However you approach the ideas in this book, I want to congratulate you for choosing to invest in your professional future by learning more about conducting business with charm and savvy. Now, you are perfectly positioned to approach your work and your business contacts with greater confidence and less hesitation. You are about to take the first step toward enjoying the many benefits of a relaxed, "correct" atmosphere that's conducive to improving productivity, profits, and the quality of your working life. By putting into practice the advice that appears here, you will:

- Gain the significant advantage over your competition that I call "the personal touch."

- Increase the likelihood that your appointments, calls, letters, and e-mail messages will receive positive attention.

- Come across as the polished professional you really are.

- Encourage others to do business with you— because they'll find doing so easy and enjoyable!

Talk to me!

Would you like to find out more about custom-tailored protocol training? Do you have a business etiquette question that is not addressed in this book? You can e-mail me at atease@eos.net. Or write to me care of At Ease, Inc., 119 East Court Street, Cincinnati, Ohio 45202. You may also call our toll-free number: 1-800-873-9909. I can assure you a prompt response.

—Ann Marie Sabath

Chapter 1

Opening Moves: Making Initial Encounters Work

"Civility costs nothing and buys everything."
—Lady Mary Wortley Montagu

Courtesy begins with introductions. If an introduction is mismanaged, there is a strong possibility that the emerging business relationship will also be subject to problems. That is why you must start right away to build a strong foundation for your new business relationships.

It probably comes as no surprise to you to learn that the initial phase of a business relationship can have extraordinary effects on careers—and on whole organizations. But who hasn't felt at least a little awkward during a business introduction? Fortunately, a few simple principles can have a dramatic, positive effect on the way you meet and greet new business associates. This chapter has eight simple principles that will help you make sure those all-important initial encounters with clients, customers, vendors, and others go as smoothly as they possibly can.

Put the ideas in this chapter into practice, and you'll have laid the groundwork for managing—and minimizing—any and all future problems. That may seem like an exaggerated claim, but the truth is that business breakthroughs are built on alliances, and alliances are built on relationships. By initiating relationships in the right way, you make later breakthroughs possible!

Tip #1
Make a super first impression.

Just as you often judge other people by the initial impact they have on you, so are you likely to be judged yourself in the first few moments of interacting with someone. Here are some tips for making a great first impression with colleagues and business associates:

- When meeting another person, extend a confident handshake as you make eye contact.

- Eliminate trendy words from your vocabulary. Modern colloquialisms may be fine on the home front, however, slang is considered inappropriate in a business environment. Thus, you should avoid a phrase such as "Awesome!" when you mean to say "Great!"

- When you are representing your organization, always carry materials (such as a briefcase, pens, and notepads) that broadcast a "quality" message. Believe it or not, supporting materials are a definite reflection of your style—and your organization's style. These materials will project an image—positive or negative—of you and your organization.

Tip #2
Know whom to introduce first.

In most situations, the basics of introductions are easy to master: Mention the name of the higher-status person first. But what if there is no higher-status person? When introducing two clients to each other, both of whom are on the same professional level, whose name should be said first?

I recommended that you say the name of the person you know least well first. By doing this, you will bring that person into the conversation and allow him or her to feel more at ease.

Tip #3
Know the value of a good handshake.

If you have ever had a strong positive or negative reaction to someone based on the firmness or weakness of the person's handshake, then you already know how important this one small gesture can be. A limp handshake can tag you as someone who is hesitant or lacking in resolution. An overpowering shake can brand you as a manipulator. A sincere, confident grip conveys confidence and authority.

Beware! People from different parts of the country expect a variety of distances between two individuals who are greeting each other. When interacting with contacts from out-of-town, try to let the other person's "space instincts" guide your approach to the handshake.

Here are a few tips for knowing how to offer a good handshake that also maintains a proper distance:

- Clasp the other person's palm with your palm, rather than fingers to fingers. Your grip should be firm. Hold someone's hand too loosely and it's possible you will earn the dreaded description of being "a dead fish."

- Do not, however, be so firm that you squeeze the other person's hand too hard. Rather than causing pain of any sort, simply apply a little pressure and then let go. Keep in mind that a handshake is not a contest to see who can grip the hardest. You should match each other, grip for grip.

- Talk to the person whose hand you are shaking; a simple "Nice to meet you" or "Good to see you again" will do.

- If you know the person well and wish to convey additional warmth, then place your free hand on top of the clasped hands or on the other person's arm or shoulder. However, do not do this if you are meeting somebody for the first time, as such a gesture can be misconstrued as an invasion of territory. If you want to convey a sense of rapport without making the other person uncomfortable, try touching his or her arm between the hand and elbow rather than between the elbow and shoulder.

- As you release the other person's hand, pause briefly but purposefully before continuing the conversation.

If you are going to another country, try to learn what the customs are there for shaking hands. In some nations it is considered polite to shake upon meeting and leaving; not doing so may give offense. For some, handshakes should be firm, for others they should be aggressive, and for still others, where there is a "caste" system, you should shake hands only with persons of a certain standing. Some countries frown on shaking hands with a member of the opposite sex. Finally, there are some social systems where the greeting is not a handshake but a bow of some sort. The more you learn about the specific customs governing these forms of greeting people, the easier it will be for you to get along, no matter what country you are in. (See the appendix for additional information on international etiquette.)

Tip #4
Manage the unconventional handshake.

When you are about to extend your hand to someone who is unable to offer you a right hand, what should you do? The first rule is—follow the other person's lead. When dealing with a person whose right hand or arm is clearly disabled, avoid reaching for that hand and pumping it energetically!

Whatever the reason for the other person's incapacity, you should issue a verbal greeting, pause, and then observe the appropriate body language and act accordingly. In some cases, the person may offer you the left hand. In other instances, the person may initiate a handshake with the right hand. The most important thing in this scenario is to let the other person set the tone.

Tip #5
Turn a social gaffe into a positive experience.

It has happened to all of us. You refer to an important client's company by his competitor's name. Or you are giving an important presentation and you make a serious misstatement. Or a gaffe you've made is pointed out to you in front of a large group.

Sooner or later, you will find yourself in an embarrassing situation that exposes you to possible ridicule or necessitates some backpedaling. Take heart: You are not alone! Blunders are a part of life. What matters is not that you've committed a *faux pas* (that's French for "misstep"), but how you handle the mistake.

Think of the situation as though it were a baseball game: An error in the field may put you behind, however, if you keep your composure, you can hit a home run in your very next at-bat and win the game.

Here are some suggested solutions for winning in embarrassing situations:

• Explain your *faux pas* with grace. Rather than getting tongue-tied with apologies, overexplaining, or trying to evade the situation, issue a concise, poised recovery. Acknowledge the misstep. Say you're sorry—then move on! For example, you may say, "Please accept my apologies for calling you by your competitor's name." Then go back to the subject at hand. When it's over, let it be over!

- Ask for help when it's needed. So you misstated something or came up blank in an assessment. Turn this to your advantage! It shows maturity to admit you are human; don't let embarrassment trip you up. For example, you may ask, "Who can help me with that particular figure?"
- Turn the attention elsewhere. The best way to do this is to praise another person. For example, you may say, "It looks like I can take a lesson or two from you!"

Any, repeat *any*, gaffe can be turned into a positive experience if it's handled with grace and wit. People remember poise! With the right approach, you won't be remembered as the person who made that mortifying blunder before a roomful of people. Instead, you'll be thought of as the person who saved the day with on-your-feet thinking and a great deal of charm!

Tip #6
Handle name lapses gracefully.

It has happened to all of us: Somebody comes up to you, greets you by name, and talks at length about how great it is to see you—and you can't place him in the least. The face may be familiar to you, but the person's name and the setting where you met eludes you completely. This situation is embarrassing, but also quite common. Believe me, it can be handled with tact and grace.

Rule number one: Do not ask, "Who are you?" Rather, respond in kind and let the person know you are glad to see him/her. One way of refreshing your memory is to ask the person what has been going on since you last talked. His or her response may reveal something (i.e., a company, a professional association, or a meeting) that will trigger the memory of how you know this person, and perhaps even his or her name.

If you still can't remember the person's name as you are talking, be cordial and simply avoid using a name of any kind. After the conversation has ended, sound out a colleague—or someone else who may have witnessed the meeting—and ask if they can help you to remember the name. (Of course, the other person may realize your predicament and, having been there himself or herself, may willingly—and sensitively—help you out by reminding you of the name.)

When it is finally revealed to you, jot down the name to help you remember it in the future and send the person a note saying that you enjoyed seeing him or her. This gesture will compensate for any discomfort associated with your not using a name when you saw each other last.

How important is taking the effort to get another person's name right?

Consider the following story. A friend of mine told me of the time he met then-Senator John F. Kennedy. Kennedy was a man who simply refused to say, "I've forgotten your name"! The senator approached my friend while they were both in the bathroom and then explained that he'd forgotten the name of someone who was waiting for him at a gathering outside. Did my friend have any ideas? Fortunately, my friend was able to provide the name of the gentleman in question, and the rest of the evening went smoothly for the senator from Massachusetts and his "old acquaintance"!

Tip #7

Use a last name unless invited to do otherwise.

One of the most common business etiquette errors is to address individuals by their first names without the other person's (stated or implicit) permission to do so. This has become an increasingly common practice in these less-formal times. Although many people have no problem moving to a "casual" conversational mode more or less instantly with new acquaintances, this practice is still unacceptable in the minds of a large number of the people you'll interact with in a business setting.

Moving to a first-name basis before the other person is ready to do so is an especially poor policy to pursue during telephone conversations with customers and prospects. Common courtesy dictates that you wait until you are invited to address a telephone contact by his or her first name—especially if the "someone" is an individual you're speaking to for the very first time. Staying with "Mr./Mrs./Ms. Smith" during phone conversations, until you're invited to use the first name, is a sound, polite business practice that should be followed at all times.

In other settings, the rule of thumb is a little more complicated. If you are meeting someone for the first time, and the other person is either a) prominent within his or her field or b) two decades older than you, you should use "Mr./Mrs./Ms." and then the last name. (In other words, even though Tiger Woods may be younger than you are, you should address him as Mr. Woods; even though Bert Rodriguez, the elderly man who delivers your mail, is not the head of the U.S. Postal Service, you should address him as Mr. Rodriguez.)

Whatever you do, refrain from asking someone permission to use a first name. Use the last name until you are directed to do otherwise. If the person wants you to move to this level of familiarity, rest assured that you'll hear about it!

Tip #8

Negotiate business card exchanges flawlessly.

During a first-time meeting, you may, as a general rule, request a business card from the other person—provided that you've offered your own card first. One exception: If the person you're speaking with is of significantly higher status (say, more than one level above your position), you should wait for the person to offer you his or her card, rather than ask for one. (Rest assured—if the senior person wants you to have a card, it will be offered to you!) Bear in mind that the more seasoned a businessperson is, the less likely he or she will be to distribute business cards or to ask for them.

You should give only one of your business cards to your contact—rather than leaving two or three. Your contact may interpret this gesture as a request from you to undertake a mass mailing. Tacky! Keep the emphasis on person-to-person contact.

Key point summary

- Make a truly positive first impression: Establish appropriate eye contact, avoid colloquialisms and slang, and have the right "support materials" at hand.

- Know who should be introduced first.

- Avoid offering a limp handshake; make sure your grip is confident and appropriate to the situation.

- Manage unconventional handshake situations by following the other person's lead.

- Remember: You can use social missteps as an opportunity to display grace, wit, and poise.

- Never ask "Who are you?"; find creative ways to determine the names of people to whom you've been introduced.

- Don't use the person's first name unless you're invited to do so.

- Present a single business card; follow the lead of a higher-ranking person, rather than asking for his or her business card.

Chapter 2

Business Dress 101: Handling Attire Problems in the Workplace

"I have heard with admiring submission the experience of the lady who declared that the sense of being perfectly well-dressed gives a feeling of inward tranquillity which religion is powerless to bestow."
—Ralph Waldo Emerson

Emerson was probably right—but the opposite is also true. Being less than perfectly well-dressed in a business setting can result in a feeling of profound discomfort that may well require therapy to dispel! And the sad truth is that "clothing mismatches" on the job can ruin the day of the person who's wearing the inappropriate attire—and the people with whom he or she comes in contact!

What can go wrong when it comes to professional attire? Plenty. In this chapter, you'll find to-the-point advice on handling the most important issues related to workplace attire. As you'll soon learn, even "casual day" wardrobe selections that carry potentially dire implications on the job can be avoided with just a minimal investment of time, care, and attention.

Know when to dress up— or dress down.

Offices vary when it comes to dress codes. Some businesses have very high standards for their employees and set strict guidelines for office attire, while others maintain a more relaxed attitude. However, it is always important to remember that no matter what your company's attitude is regarding what you wear, you are working in a business environment and you should dress accordingly. This applies not only to business casual wear but to more formal business attire, as well. Certain items may be more appropriate for evening wear than for a business meeting, just as shorts and a T-shirt are better suited for the beach than for an office environment.

Your attire should reflect both your environment and your position. A senior vice president has a different image to maintain than that of a secretary or sales assistant.

Like it or not, you can and will be judged by your personal appearance!

This is never more apparent than on "dress-down days," when what you wear can say more about you than any business suit ever could. In fact, people will pay *more* attention to what you wear on dress-down days than on "business professional" days! Thus, when dressing in "business casual" clothes, try to put some flair into your wardrobe choices; recognize that the "real" definition of business casual is to dress just one notch down from what you would normally wear on business-professional attire days. Avoid jeans, worn, wrinkled polo shirts, sneakers, scuffed shoes, halter tops, and revealing blouses. For men, try wearing a neat pair of pants and a buttoned shirt with long or short sleeves that has more color or texture in the fabric. For women, wear skirts or tailored pants with blouses, blazers, and accessories that mean business yet convey a more casual look than your standard business attire.

One simple, never-to-be-violated rule that applies to both men and women: Avoid wearing clothes that reveal too much or leave little to the imagination! For example, men who wear shorts to the office—even on Saturdays—may unintentionally signal to others that they don't recognize standards for appropriate business casual dress. The same rule holds true for women who wear skirts that are tighter and shorter than "business professional" skirts. Why risk the chance of not being taken seriously by managers and colleagues?

Remember, there are boundaries between your career and your social life. You should dress one way for play and another way when you mean business.

Always ask yourself where you're going and how other people will be dressed when you get there. Is the final destination the opera, the beach, or the office? Dress accordingly, and you will discover the truth in the axiom that clothes make the man—and the woman! When in doubt, always err on the side of dressing slightly more conservatively than the situation demands. Remember, you can always remove a jacket, but you can't put one on if you didn't think to take it with you!

Tip #10
Avoid overaccessorizing.

Whether you are a man or a woman, the way in which you use accessories reveals a great deal about you. Accessories can communicate who and what you are as a person, in the way you are presenting yourself and in your attention to detail.

The most common opportunity for overaccessorizing is probably to be found in jewelry. In this case, the basic rule of thumb in a business environment is that less is more. Earrings on men are strictly taboo; women should choose earrings that are simple yet elegant and should wear no more than one pair. Pins provide nice accents to a business ensemble, yet they need not be the main attention-grabber. Be tuned into your organization's culture to decide whether or not you can wear multiple-bangle bracelets; in some workplaces they are considered inappropriate. For both sexes, "appropriate" in a professional setting means wearing a maximum of one ring on each hand, worn on either the ring finger or the pinkie.

Tip #11
Skip the cheap accessories.

Make sure that (for instance) the business pen you carry portrays a positive professional image. When dressed professionally, avoid carrying a plastic pen, just as you would avoid wearing a Power Rangers watch with a plastic band.

While you're investing in a decent-looking pen, you should also take note of your briefcase, luggage, and umbrella. Are they as well-maintained as they can possibly be? Do they look sharp? Or can they stand to be replaced? If a "maybe" even popped into your mind, get out there and invest in some new stuff that will pay big dividends for your career.

Tip #12
If you're an employer, clarify "business casual attire."

Some companies set up a "dress-down day" policy, then forget to tell the employees exactly what they mean by "dress-down." Unpleasant sartorial surprises sometimes arise as a result!

If you are the person responsible for creating a policy and procedure manual—or at the very least, a detailed memo—that describes specifically what you do and don't want to see on business casual days. By doing this, you'll give your people guidelines to follow and help them plan that (often tricky) "third wardrobe."

Remember to mention the basics: If you want men to wear shoes and socks instead of open-toed sandals and women to wear hosiery with dresses, even if they have a great tan, say so. By taking a few simple steps to formalize the boundaries of business casual day, you can clarify what is and isn't acceptable, keep your working environment professional, and avoid the strange looks from important visitors when your work force as a whole looks like it just returned from Schlockville, U.S.A.

Tip #13

Refer to "the Book" to solve attire problems among subordinates.

Recently, I received a call from a personnel director who wanted to know how to approach a woman who wore sleeveless blouses to work (whose bra and slip straps always seemed to show). The caller wanted to know how she could get this person to change the way she dressed, without shattering her ego?

I suggested that she appropriately update the organization's procedure manual to include a business casual code (see Tip #12) and that she depersonalize the exchange by taking a "rules are rules" approach during a private (and low-key) meeting. It worked!

Did you ever see the cover of that Dilbert book, *Casual Day Has Gone Too Far?* The scene, of course, is a modern office on "business casual day." In addition to various strangely dressed employees, a nude cartoon character—presumably an envelope-pushing employee—walks calmly among the maze of cubicles. You may not have to deal with problems like that on a regular basis on casual day. However, it's entirely possible that you will have to contend with outfits that leave far too little to the imagination, excessive jewelry, T-shirts that display offensive messages, or any number of other "creative" attire choices that draw not just second glances, but gasps of disbelief.

In other words, there's a very good chance that today's managers will have to contend with fashion statements that send the wrong message—loudly—to colleagues, visiting clients, and last but not least, The Big Boss. In cases where you're looking at major provocations, rather than minor misunderstandings of the company dress code on casual day, your best bet is to pull the person aside, find a place for a private discussion, and explain the nature of the problem sensitively yet directly. Your cause will be considerably easier if you have a written dress code that outlines exactly what is and is not acceptable on casual day. Begin by telling the person that he or she is a valued employee. Then explain—without making accusations or casting aspersions on the other person's style—that casual day is a tricky thing and that the way the company has attempted to avoid confusion is by stating what it considers appropriate in its handouts and printed materials. Let the offender know that the company needs his or her assistance now— that it's time to go home to change into *business* casual attire, rather than the "casual" and inappropriate garment(s) he or she is currently wearing. Specify exactly what's "over the line": a halter top, a see-through blouse, Bermuda shorts, a miniskirt. Be specific, rather than assuming that the person can read your mind. Whether the person lives 10 minutes from work or an hour, you should take this action. Why? It will set the necessary precedent, relaying to other employees that rules are meant to be followed and if they are not, changes will have to be made.

Tip #14

Make sure your casual dress says that *you* mean business.

Is there a bigger workplace *faux pas* than showing up seriously underdressed for work because you had a different idea of what "business casual day" meant than everyone else did? Well, yes, there probably is, however that doesn't mean you shouldn't concern yourself with staying on the right side of this potentially tricky issue if you're not in a position to formulate clear written guidelines yourself.

How casual is your organization's business casual day? The answer varies from company to company, of course, and, alas, not all companies develop formal written guidelines for the benefit of employees. One thing is for certain, though. You will never get in trouble for being too underdressed on business casual days if you follow this simple rule: Change your regular professional attire by only a single garment.

For example, men, if your organization's culture requires that you wear a suit on "business professional days," wear a sport coat on business casual days. And for women, swap that conservative blouse you wear on most days with a knit top that is compatible with your blazer.

By following this simple (and, yes, conservative) rule when dressing business casual, you'll still be able to go to a last-minute client meeting on a moment's notice—without having to apologize for how you look. I've been asked many times whether it's acceptable for women to wear slacks on dress-down days in professional environments where this would otherwise be considered inappropriate. The (frustrating) answer is: It depends on the culture of the organization for which you work. The safest standard is probably to keep an eye on what the highest-ranking woman in your organization does and follow her example.

Key point summary

- Don't pick clothes that reveal too much or leave too little to the imagination. And when in doubt, always err on the side of dressing slightly more conservatively than the situation demands.

- Keep accessories to a tasteful minimum.

- Don't opt for chintzy-looking accessories.

- If you're the boss, make it clear exactly what "casual attire" means in your workplace.

- Avoid pointless conflicts—pull errant or inappropriately dressed employees aside, and have a low-key "rules are rules" meeting about company attire standards. (Make sure there's something down in black and white for you to point to!)

- Still stumped about what to wear? Try this rule: Change your regular professional attire by only a single garment.

Chapter 3

Correspondence: Putting It Down in Black and White

"This morning I took out a comma and this afternoon I put it back in again."
—Oscar Wilde

It would certainly be nice if we all had the kind of schedule that allowed for the leisurely approach to writing that Mr. Wilde seemed prepared to follow. But in today's business world, where deadlines are tight, budgets are tighter, and more people than ever act as their own "secretary," the truth is that we're spread thinner than ever. That means that we have to learn how to develop written correspondence that makes the right first impression—in a hurry—and avoid the careless errors that can (and do) lose companies business.

In this chapter, you find out how to make sure the written documents you prepare in a business setting look as sharp as they possibly can. You'll get important advice on using proper English, formatting your letters and reports correctly, and addressing your intended reader in the right way. You'll also get some invaluable advice on preparing and sending communications via fax, e-mail, newsgroup postings, and overnight courier.

Is it worth your while to bother about putting a comma where it belongs? You'd better believe it is. Thankfully, though, once you've assimilated the easy-to-follow, easy-to-execute advice that appears here, you'll be in a great position to make your correspondence "letter perfect"—without spending an entire day pondering a single sentence.

Tip #15
Brush up your English.

Many people place a high importance on a well-written letter or document—and rightfully so. Not only does proper grammar and spelling increase the likelihood of a positive response to the message contained in any piece of writing, it also demonstrates your own care and attention to detail. If you send out a letter that is rife with misspellings and grammatical errors, you will present yourself as someone who doesn't care enough to proofread—or simply doesn't care about the basics of good writing.

Reacquaint yourself with the basic rules of grammar and style. Read *The Elements of Style*, by Strunk and White, if you're looking for a concise review of the most important rules.

Use the spell check in your word processing program to catch any spelling errors you might have missed, but make sure it's proofread by a qualified human being, too. (Spell checkers have a way of passing over errors such as "two much time" or "wind-win situation.")

In addition:

- Take care in capitalizing names and titles. Consult a style guide, such as *The Chicago Manual of Style,* if you are uncertain about the approach you should take.

- As much as possible, use the active voice ("John will write the memo") rather than the passive voice ("The memo will be written by John"). The active voice adds strength, brevity, and definition to your sentence structure.

- Avoid using incomplete or run-on sentences. Write in complete sentences that have a subject and a verb.

- Check your document carefully for punctuation. Make sure it's been used properly and is consistent throughout the piece.

If the document is an important one and you feel uncertain about your grammatical skills, you will probably want to get feedback from more than one source on your spelling, grammar, and punctuation. The more care you take, the better your document or letter—and therefore you—will be received.

Tip #16
Make sure your document looks sharp.

Here are just a few simple guidelines for creating a professional-looking document:

- Avoid using too many typefaces. Today's word processors make it possible for you to set up a letter that features, say, six or seven fonts. Such a document is likely to leave the recipient's head spinning! A good rule of thumb: Pick one "display" font for headlines and subheadings, and one "text" font for the main body of your message.

- Keep it (relatively) formal. Remember that you are writing something that will be received by a business colleague, not a friend. So go easy on any personal touches ("Hiya Bill," or "Let's confab pronto, buddy!") you may be tempted to inject.

- Be consistent in your formatting. If you indent the beginning of your paragraphs, then indent them throughout the document. If you highlight text by using italics, avoid switching to underlining later. Take care that titles and spellings (especially spellings of proper names), are consistent. Avoid referring to someone as Ms. Roderigo in one line—and Mrs. Rodderigo in the next.

- Avoid cramming a single page with too much text. Again, modern word processing programs may let you fit vast amounts of type on a page if you jam everything into six-point type. But would you want to read such a document? Once again—proofread! Aside from grammar, punctuation, and spelling, you may have accidentally omitted a word or two, or included something that is best deleted.

Tip #17

Use the proper salutation.

When writing a business letter, be formal with your opening, especially if you are writing to someone outside the country. A proper, formal salutation is essential to any business correspondence. Letters that begin with an improper or nonexistent greeting may offend the receiver.

To begin, make sure your letter is formatted at the top with the date and the name and full address of the person to whom you are writing. Your salutation line should be two spaces below the last line of the address (or below the reference line, if there is one). At this point, the question arises: Do you use the last name with the appropriate title or the first name of the person you are writing to? Unless you are already on a first-name basis with your addressee, always use the formal mode of address—i.e., "Dear Mr. Smith" or "Dear Ms. Jones." Your salutation line should then end with a colon, which is the preferred practice in most business correspondence.

Rules for writing business letters vary from country to country. Professional translation services should be familiar with conventions for opening and closing corporate correspondence in countries outside the United States. They'll also assist with such conventions as the addressing of envelopes and the proper use of names and titles. If you're uncertain about the procedure you should follow in drafting a letter to an international contact and you don't have access to a translation service, your best bet may be to check your own files for samples of correspondence from the country—or call the nation's embassy for suggestions.

Tip #18
Address spouses by their proper titles.

Marriage may not be as simple as it once was—and neither is addressing letters or invitations to married couples, especially in a time of reevaluation of traditional gender roles. The stay-at-home wife is a rarity these days. You are more likely to find that both spouses work outside the home and that one or both hold professional degrees. So what does this mean for our traditional methods of addressing a letter (i.e., "Mr. and Mrs. George Smith")? Here is a guide to help you:

- When one or both are doctors:

  Dr. and Mrs. George Smith

  or

  Dr. Mary Smith and Mr. George Smith

  or

  Dr. Mary Smith and Dr. George Smith

- When one or both are Reverends:

  The Reverend George Smith and Mrs. Smith

  or

  The Reverend Mary Smith and Mr. George Smith

  or

  The Reverend Mary Smith and The Reverend George Smith

- When a woman uses her own name (or the couple is not married):

  Ms. (or Dr.) Mary Jones and Mr. (or Dr.) George Smith

Tip #19

Make fax, e-mail, and overnight mail guarantees.

Does what you're sending "absolutely, positively" have to reach its destination by a certain time?

When faxing or sending a document "overnight" or via courier, let the receiver know that you are a person of your word. Give the person a realistic time estimate of when the information will be received. If you know that you can have the information to the person by a given time (i.e., within an hour via fax or courier or by 10:30 a.m. the next business morning via Federal Express, UPS, etc.), take personal responsibility for the shipment! Say, "I will personally see to it that you receive the package via [fax/courier/overnight] by [whatever time]. If you don't have the materials by that time, please let me know." Here's a variation that allows you to take ownership for following up on a fax transmission. Say, "I will fax this information to you by 5 p.m. today. You will also receive a voice mail from me to confirm the time it was sent." Then call as you'd promised. This step will virtually remove the possibility that your transmission will "slip through the cracks."

Tip #20

Follow up on "special deliveries" after you've made the guarantee.

When faxing a document or sending something via overnight mail or by courier, monitoring its progress is crucial! Ensure that the package was received safely by taking appropriate follow-up measures. This not only keeps the lines of communication open, but it reassures the receiver that you are taking care of the document's safe delivery. It also lets the receiver know that you are a person of your word.

Make the call!

Tip #21

Include a cover letter with "impersonal" written materials.

Rather than sending that contract "cold"—add some warmth! It may help you win or retain a customer. Always include a cover letter with checks, legal documents, proposals, or other written materials. The cover page adds warmth and personality to what otherwise may be perceived as an impersonal enclosure. Another great way to add a personal touch to your cover letter is to sign it with a blue fountain pen. (Black may be mistaken for a preprinted signature.) If you can, add a postscript that refers to something personal your contact mentioned to you. For example: "Hope you have a great vacation!" or "Hope you enjoy *The Phantom of the Opera* this weekend as much as we did!"

Tip #22

Provide sufficient information in e-mail messages.

"Yes! Yes! I want to set up a meeting to discuss what you outlined in your e-mail message, however, I don't have your phone number! Get back to me immediately or we'll have to call the whole thing off!"

If ever there was a message that wasn't supposed to linger unanswered in your electronic mailbox, that's the one. The truth is, though, it never should have been written in the first place. Any business contact with whom you conduct e-mail correspondence should be able to pick up the phone and call you or fax you something or drop an overnight package into the local pickup box—without having to rely on another e-mail message from you.

Unlike "snail mail," e-mail can usually be answered immediately with the click of a few keys or a button on your mouse. On most systems, you don't even need to remember—or even notice—the sender's e-mail address. Once you read the message, you can type a few words of your own in response, hit the "reply" command, and send your answer hurtling back through cyberspace.

But suppose the person you're in touch with wants to enter all your relevant contact information into his or her personal database?

Frequently, users of e-mail forget to include the contact information that will make later communication possible. If a contact decides to mail you a brochure, proposal, or formal bid request, it will be a challenge for him or her to do so if there's no street address at the end of your message.

Similarly, if the person with whom you're corresponding decides that it's important to get in contact with you immediately, he or she probably won't appreciate having to wait until you next check your e-mail. (Be honest, sometimes you let it slip for a couple of days.) A fax will at least be noticed immediately, and even a phone message has an immediacy that e-mail distinctly lacks.

If you care enough about the business relationship to correspond in the first place, make a point of including all your relevant contact information at the conclusion of your message.

Tip #23
Observe e-mail courtesy.

It is a fact of modern life that e-mail is increasingly replacing standard letters and memos—even phones and faxes—as a form of fast, easy, inexpensive, and effective communication. However, many people have not yet mastered the basic etiquette for sending concise and courteous messages electronically. In many cases, e-mail has become just as necessary to establishing rapport with a customer or colleague as face-to-face interaction.

However, e-mail has a potential disadvantage—it's both informal (like telephone conversations) and one-sided (like standard business correspondence). E-mail *feels* casual, almost as casual as spoken discourse, yet it often lacks the nuance or personality that is normally conveyed by voice inflections and body language. That means e-mail has the potential of creating miscommunication that may be difficult to undo once you hit the "send" button. The stakes can be quite high, which makes proper e-mail etiquette a must. Here are a few basic rules to follow:

- Make sure your subject heading is clear. Your electronic mail recipient may be wading through a pile of e-mail messages (much of it unsolicited sales-related material), and will be selective about the ones she or he wants to read by the subject heading. You'll want your e-mail message to stand out from the others in the "in" box by its contents and importance. Avoid leaving the subject heading blank. Make sure it isolates exactly what you're talking about that's of interest to your reader! For example: "Schedule for your Atlanta trip."

- Address the receiver by name in the opening sentence and do so properly. Good "Netiquette" dictates that you simply include the receiver's name in the first sentence (i.e., "Mary, thank you for sending me that report."). In addition, follow simple rules of courtesy in your opening. For instance, address chief executives, customers, and people you don't know as "Mr.," "Ms.," "Mrs.," or "Dr." unless permission has already been given to address them by their first names.

- Devise an electronic "signature." Because your message is not on official company stationery, create a "sign-off" that includes your full name and all other relevant information. (See Tip #22 on including contact information in e-mail messages.) A brief slogan, vision statement, or quote can also be added, as long as it is professionally oriented and displays good taste.

- Keep your message as concise as possible. Unless you're passing along information that has been specifically requested by your recipient, try to keep your e-mail to a maximum of two screens. (Remember, by the time your message reaches its intended recipient, it may have a half-screen or more of electronic gobbledygook appended to the top of the message.)

- When replying to another person, quote excerpts (or, for short messages, the entire text) of the original communication. This releases you from the necessity of summarizing or reiterating what the other person has written. Furthermore, you will remind the receiver of his or her original request and spare the person from pulling up the original message for review.

- Tailor your message for the receiver. Writing to the CEO of a company with whom you hope to do business is not the same as writing to a co-worker or supplier who happens to be a personal friend! While an informal, chatty tone is acceptable in the latter case, it should be avoided when writing to company executives or customers. Your e-mail message should maintain the same degree of professionalism that exists when sending correspondence on company letterhead.

- Maintain confidentiality. Treat your electronic correspondence with the same respect that you do any business letter or memo. Refrain from sharing or forwarding an e-mail unless given permission to do so by the original sender.

• Use proper spelling and grammar. Even an electronic message should be properly formatted and checked for spelling or grammatical errors. Many online services now provide spell-checking for e-mail compositions; virtually all of them will allow you to import text from your word processor. Once you've spell-checked the message, proofread it carefully before sending it, or suffer the consequences when a gaffe you've made costs you embarrassment—or your company dollars.

• Check your electronic mailbox at least once a day. More often than not, people send e-mails to each other because they are looking for a quick response. Check your in-box as often as possible in order to acknowledge messages received.

• Respond in a timely manner. Whether it's a phone call or an e-mail, no one likes to be kept waiting, and certainly not your e-mail correspondent. Send a reply as quickly as you can, preferably within 24 hours, even if it's just to say you have received the message and will follow up. If your e-mail program is capable of doing so, provide for an "automatic reply" whenever you are away—a message that automatically acknowledges receipt of messages and provides information about when you will return.

Tip #24

Don't mix e-business with e-pleasure.

Keep your personal e-mail messages out of the workplace. If this is a problem, set up a private e-mail account for your home use.

When you're at work, you should be working. Corresponding with a long-lost buddy from college (usually) is not what you're paid to do. So separate the two worlds!

Using the office e-mail system to circulate jokes, pass along nonwork-related gossip, or conduct other private correspondence is unethical and may cost you your job! It can usually be tracked—even if you press "delete" after sending your message. All the "Powers That Be" have to do is go back to the master tape. (And remember, your company may be liable for information—or disinformation—that "leaks" into the far reaches of cyberspace inadvertently.)

Think before you key! If you wouldn't want the message to be posted on your company bulletin board, don't send it through the e-mail system. Play it safe and conduct personal e-mail correspondence at home. Conduct work-related e-mail correspondence at work.

Tip #25

Follow the rules of good "Netiquette."

E-mail—a message passed from one electronic mailbox to another—is only one way of communicating electronically.

Online interactions can also take place through other modes of the Internet, for instance, electronic "bulletin boards," news groups, and discussion groups.

It is difficult enough to communicate electronically on a one-on-one basis, but posting to a group can sometimes create misunderstandings that cause unintended offense to someone within the group. Therefore, a few Netiquette tips are in order:

- Be brief and to the point. Most people don't have the time or inclination to read lengthy postings.

- Provide a descriptive subject heading that gives a clear idea of your subject. This allows others to decide whether or not they want to read your message.

- When replying to another message or posting, quote the material to which you are responding so that others within the group can be clued in to your subject.

- The advice on avoiding the overuse of CAPITAL LETTERS is just as pertinent here as in one-on-one e-mail.

- Use care in the tone of your messages and, if it's helpful to you, use "emoticons." Humor and sarcasm often can be misinterpreted. If you are trying to convey a certain tone, employ an electronic hieroglyphic that sends a nonverbal message. For instance, :-) means "Get it?" or "Just joking," and ;-) is a wink. On the other hand, :-(demonstrates sadness or disappointment, and <g> is a grin, to indicate that you are "just teasing." Emphasis or italics can be conveyed by the use of *asterisks*.

There are other emoticons and symbols to convey a wide range of emotions, although they should be used with discretion. (Relying too heavily on these symbols can lead to messages that are a little too cute for their own good!)

- When posting to a discussion group, make sure that your message is pertinent to the group's topic. Many members of a group will dislike the intrusion of any message that is considered to be "off-topic" or a repetition of topics or questions that have been asked and answered many times previously. If the group has a FAQ (a list of Frequently Asked Questions), consult it before sending a message or question online.

- Include a signature at the end of your messages that gives your name, company, and e-mail address.

Key point summary

- Track down a copy of *The Elements of Style*. Read it from cover to cover, and keep it by your desk at all times.

- Use both your spell check and a human set of eyes to ensure that your document is free of spelling mistakes. Check it carefully for grammar problems, too.

- Format your document intelligently—don't cram it with lots of competing typefaces, adopt an inappropriate informal tone, follow your own rules inconsistently, or jam too much text onto the page.

- Make sure your document incorporates the right salutation for the intended reader.

- Addressing a letter to people who are married or who consider each other "significant others"? Don't tick off one or both of your intended readers; use the proper titles for the pair you're addressing.

- Make promises you can keep when it comes to sending faxes, e-mail transmissions, and overnight packages.

- Call afterwards to make sure that what you sent arrived in one piece.

- Remember to send a cover letter when enclosing "impersonal" materials.

- Include all your relevant contact information at the conclusion of an e-mail message.

- Know the ins and outs of e-mail composition.

- Keep personal e-mail transmissions out of the workplace.

- When posting to Internet groups, make sure you observe the rules of good "Netiquette" by, for instance, only sending messages that are pertinent to the group and quoting excerpts of previously posted material when the need arises.

Chapter 4

Sound Advice: Making the Right Phone Impression

*"Nature has given men one tongue and two ears,
that we may hear twice as much as we speak."*
—Epictetus

Somehow the fact that people have two ears doesn't always keep them from talking over, under, around, and through the individuals they encounter during business calls. Haven't you had phone contact with some organization or other that left you feeling as though you'd been consciously ignored, insulted, or both?

If there is a potentially devastating "profit vacuum" that this book can help you overcome quickly and easily, it's the common error of treating people on the phone as though they weren't entitled to a full hearing. There's a rash of phone-related etiquette problems in the business world today, and who can say how many millions of dollars in lost revenue from clients and customers it's costing us?

All I know for sure is that when a company is rude to me over the phone, it doesn't take me long to start thinking about moving my business elsewhere.

In this chapter, you'll learn the best ways to establish and maintain proper communication over the phone. By following the tips outlined here, you'll help your organization *build* bridges during phone contacts, rather than tear them down.

Tip #26
Ask before putting someone on speakerphone.

Looking for a great way to lose (or, at the very least, intimidate) a big customer? Call your contact person's direct number while you and one or more associates are already "on speaker." When the person picks up the ringing phone and says "Hello," he or she will be greeted by a cavernous rush of responding static-sound that may or may not include a distinguishable human voice at its center. Instead of wondering about how on earth you've managed to pull off the latest customer service miracle, your contact will wonder what terrible transgression he or she committed to earn a spot in Telephonic Hell. You thought there was nothing worse than making a client listen to the Muzak version of "Something" while a call is transferred? Guess again.

There are very few devices that register as much displeasure from unsuspecting phone users as the speakerphone. If you're using it, this technology represents a superb and welcome convenience. If you're subjected to it without warning, however, it's among the rudest of rude telephone awakenings. Many listeners report that they feel as though the other person is talking to them from the bottom of a well during speakerphone conversations. The instinct to shout (or hang up in the hope of securing a better connection) can be quite strong.

Sound phone etiquette requires that the person who wishes to use the speakerphone always pick up the handset first when calling another party. After greeting the person on the line and establishing rapport, the person with the speakerphone should explain why he or she would like to put the call on this device. For instance: "George Smith, who is our firm's director of communications, is in my office. I think he'd benefit from your feedback. If it's all right with you, I'd like to put this call on speakerphone." Most callers won't mind—as long as the switch over is discussed before it is initiated and the benefit to the caller of placing the call on speakerphone is made clear.

What should you do when you find yourself in a telephone conversation in which the other person does not ask your permission to put you on the speakerphone? You have two options: Tolerate the lapse in sound quality (and remind yourself that your communications are not confidential), or explain that you cannot hear the person well and hope that this will encourage the other party to use the handset instead.

Tip #27
Observe proper conference call etiquette.

Yes, there is a certain etiquette to be observed when conducting or taking part in a conference call. Any situation that involves other people, in fact, requires thoughtful consideration of anybody else who might be involved. This is true whether the interactions are in person or by some electronic means.

The primary responsibility for a conference call obviously lies with the person who is organizing it. First and foremost, the participants in the call must be notified in advance of the date. This action should serve to verify whether they are available to participate in the call, as well as to ensure that it is noted on their calendars. The organizer should then follow up via e-mail or fax to confirm the day and time and to provide a list of who will be participating in the call.

When announcing the time of the conference call, the time zone should be included. If an out-of-country participant will be involved, the call should be arranged with the time difference firmly in mind. In addition to a general announcement, an agenda should be sent to each person prior to the date of the call. The agenda allows each person to learn the goals of the telephone meeting and what his or her involvement will be.

The call will usually fall into one of two categories: Either you will be calling all involved parties and connecting them via your own phone system, or they will be required to call a certain number themselves to connect to the conference call. If your call falls into the latter category, you must make absolutely certain that your memo providing the meeting details includes everything a participant needs to know to be connected to the call.

As with any other meeting, punctuality is key to a conference call. Whether you are the organizer or a participant, you should be at your phone at the appointed hour. If you have organized the call, you must also observe certain etiquette in getting others on the line. The first person should be called within five minutes before the designated time; the last person should be called a minute or so before the meeting is scheduled to begin.

Those who are "lowest on the totem pole" should be connected first; the most senior executive or client should be connected last. If the meeting requires the other participants to call in themselves to be connected, you should ensure that all involved parties are on the line before commencing the meeting.

Once everyone is connected, the conference call host should greet the group as a whole and introduce all other persons on the line, who should then acknowledge their presence with a short greeting (i.e., "Hello" or "Good morning"). Once this basic courtesy is out of the way, the meeting should commence according to the agenda that had been previously distributed.

One major difficulty with conference calls is, of course, the inability to see your fellow callers. This prevents you from tuning into the body language that may indicate when another person wants to speak. In addition, people who talk out of turn may interrupt or drown out the caller who "has the floor." It can be extremely disconcerting to have several people talking at the same time. The calls tend to run most smoothly when one person determines whose turn it is to talk next—and when others refrain from speaking until they are asked for input.

When it is time to end the call, the host should provide a summary of no more than a few sentences, describing what was discussed and/or decided. After the call has ended, the host or the person who has been designated to take notes should promptly send a follow-up letter to each member of the group to confirm any action plan that had been discussed and to outline the responsibilities of each person in the group.

Tip #28

Keep people who field calls for you informed.

"Hello, Mr. Smith's office."

"This is Mr. Big. Is he there?"

"I'm sorry, he isn't. May I take a message?"

"No, it's too important. When will he be back?"

"I'm afraid I don't know."

"Well, do you know where I can reach him?"

"Sorry, no. May I give him a message?"

"No, I need to talk to him before 3 p.m. or we'll lose this account."

One of the most frustrating experiences a caller can have in trying to get through to you is talking to someone who cannot provide any information on your schedule or availability. Many managers, in fact, prefer to keep their own schedules without bothering to fill in their subordinates concerning their whereabouts. What they don't realize is that by saving themselves that time and trouble, they can often create time and trouble for others.

Learn to use your office support staff effectively, particularly those people who represent you when you are out of the office. Your administrative assistants should be aware of both your schedule and any important projects you are working on that may require them to "run interference" for you when you are away. To this end, it is important to always provide a copy of your schedule so that your assistant(s) may know where you are and how to contact you when you are the only person who can handle a situation. You even may provide a script of what to say when you are out of the office, such as, "Ms. Jones is in a client meeting this morning and will return to her office this afternoon. May I help you or would you like to leave a detailed message on her voice mail?"

Also, give assistants both the responsibility of taking your calls and the authority to let callers know when they can expect a call back. ("Mr. Smith will return to his office this afternoon. May I have him call you back later today?")

Any information that an assistant might need for callers should also be provided: "Ms. Jones is not in the office right now, however she asked me to let you know that you'll be getting that report first thing tomorrow morning." When calls are treated in this manner, it demonstrates your ability to work as a team with your assistants and coworkers, as well as to respect the callers' time.

Tip #29
Avoid the most common telephone *faux pas.*

The wooing, winning, and retention of customers usually means relying on salespeople who know the product or service being sold and can conduct themselves in a courteous, professional manner. Frequently, much of a salesperson's business must be conducted over the telephone. It is important for salespeople to avoid certain telephonic *faux pas* that can adversely affect the relationship with the customer or potential customer. Truth be told, however, anyone and everyone can benefit from telephone courtesy.

Here are some tips that will help keep calls on the right track:

- Plan the call before you make it—rather than improvising on the line. Before you start dialing, mentally prepare for the call by jotting down the questions you'd like to ask and the information you'd like to share.

- Make sure you have close to hand all the information and resources you'll need. That includes your calendar, a copy of the proposal or other sales material you sent to the person, data on customers in the same industry, a file containing any information you have on this contact, and a pad and pen. If you know you're going to need to track down information that will necessitate a round of telephone tag, wait to make the call until you have it assembled.

- Avoid calling when you know your client or contact is likely to feel overwhelmed. If you know the person you're calling has to deal with a rush at work between 4:30 and 5:30 each day, don't try to make a sales call to the person during this period. If you know your customer or prospective customer has just returned from vacation, avoid calling the first day he or she is back in the office.

- Come up for air once in a while during the conversation. If you're going to hold a monologue, why call the person in the first place? Make your point in a concise manner and then give the other person the chance to talk.

- Take careful notes during the conversation, so that your customer doesn't have to repeat remarks or provide important information twice. By doing so, you'll be demonstrating your efficiency and attention to detail.

Tip #30
Be kind to fellow travelers.

Telephones and their electronic cousins are so much a part of modern life that it's easy to take them for granted. From the basic handset to cordless phones to cellular phones to beepers, modern technology allows us constant access to the rest of the world. These days, it is common to see people walking down the street with telephones to their ears or carrying on conversations while driving their cars. But is it really appropriate to conduct business calls anywhere? We are so used to telephones that many of us forget how serious lapses in telephone courtesy can be.

Many of the most common breaches of etiquette occur on airplanes. Avoid using air phones to conduct long, nonemergency business conversations. First and foremost, it's expensive—and if there's anything the accounting department considers impolite, it's a huge expense! Secondly, long discourses during extended flights are inconsiderate.

Your telephone calls are of little interest or concern to your fellow passengers. In fact, it is unfair to subject them at length to your business affairs unless you have absolutely no choice. Air phones are best used for emergencies or when nobody else is within three rows of you.

Tip #31
Watch that beeper.

Avoid using beepers that "sound off." This can be worse than the sound of someone belching in public! Overloud paging is noise pollution at its worst and (unfortunately) is still used by many as a conscious, and clumsy, symbol of self-importance. To avoid bothering others, especially in public places, get a "silent" beeper that vibrates when you have a call.

Tip #32
Set limits to personal calls at your home office.

Don't allow friends to assume that just because you work at home, you are free to take phone calls. Treat such calls the same way you would if your manager was standing right next to you in an office. Simply say, "It's good to hear from you. May I get back to you this evening?" You also may use your answering machine or Caller ID to screen your calls for you.

Tip # 33

Personalize your voice mail.

It's a fact of modern life. Often, the person who is trying to reach you by phone will not be able to do so because you are either on the phone already or away from your desk. Therefore, unless you have an assistant to take messages for you, the chances are good that your voice mail will click in on your behalf. Voice mail is, in effect, your private assistant. It is an extension of you and should reflect the same basic courtesy and regard for others that you would demonstrate in person. To this end, I recommend that you keep your voice mail message updated regularly. This will let callers know when you are out of the office and/or when they might expect to get a call back from you.

You may "personalize" your greeting, but that does not mean making it funny or adding sound effects. Your greeting should be professional and to the point. For example:

"Thank you for your call. I am at a client site today and will return to the office tomorrow. If you need immediate attention, please dial Mary Smith at extension 123. Otherwise, please leave your name, telephone number, and message. I will return your call promptly tomorrow."

Tip #34

Learn to let the phone ring.

It's true: Answer your telephone only when you *can* talk. If the time is not right for you, most callers would prefer to leave a voice message if the alternatives are either to be rushed through the call or to hear you say that you only have enough time to tell them you don't have enough time to talk.

The same principle applies during meetings. If the only thing you'll be saying to the caller who interrupts a get-together is that you can't talk just now, let the call go into voice mail. You'll be saving time (and preventing aggravation) for three people: the person in your office, the caller, and yourself!

Tip #35
Check your voice mail and e-mail regularly.

Technology's great, but only if you keep up with it!

Some people make a point of checking voice mail and e-mail messages two to three times a day. Others find that less frequent check-ins are sufficient for the work they do. Find the level that makes sense for you—it should be at least once a day—rather than letting messages linger unattended.

These days, no matter how involved you are in what you are doing, you are expected to get back to others promptly—by the next day at the latest. That's one of the implications of modern communications technology: A three- or four-day lag between an initial message and response, which not too long ago was tolerated, is now considered unacceptable.

Tip #36
Be specific when
leaving a phone message.

"Hi, this is Tom Smith. Call me." (Click)

Would you like to receive a telephone message such as this? The problems with it are obvious. Aside from being too abrupt (and therefore rude), there is no telephone number provided. More importantly, it lacks a real message.

What is the call about? What, if anything, should you have ready when you return the call?

Rather than leaving a vague phone message, always provide a reason for your call, even if it's personal. This allows the other person to prepare for the callback, thus making it more likely that you will hear from him or her promptly and lessen the possibility of your entering into a game of "telephone tag."

Here are more helpful hints for leaving a message that is specific and ensures a timely response:

- Provide a brief but detailed idea of what you are calling about: "I need to discuss the Rollins account with you. Can we set up a meeting?" or "I'm looking for that report you promised to send me."

- Give your message a time frame: "Can you give me five minutes to discuss this?" or "I need to get your marketing figures before our presentation next Tuesday."

- If you are trying to reach a prospective client, include a "what's in it for you" message: "Please contact me so I can tell you how you can save time processing orders."
- Add a teaser that will make the other party want to return your call: "I may have found the solution to your personnel problem."
- Always leave your phone number! Just because you have talked to this person before doesn't mean that he or she has your number immediately at hand. Save the other party the time and effort of looking up your number by including it with your message.

Tip #37

Get to the point when leaving voice mail messages.

Use voice mail economically, especially when you're leaving an update or an important fact. Respect the other person's time. Keep it short and sweet. (And remember, some message systems operate with a time limit!)

You may want to "rehearse" your message ahead of time:

"Hi, Ellen, this is Brenda at 212-555-2222. Just wanted to let you know that I got your e-mail transmission this morning. I'll call back this afternoon once I've had the chance to go over your comments in detail."

Tip #38

Explain the
reason for your call.

How do you feel when you're in the middle of an important, time-sensitive project at work and someone calls to talk to you, seemingly about nothing in particular?

If you're like most of us, you feel a bit of resentment when you have to deal with such calls. So don't make them yourself! When contacting another person by phone, always explain the reason for your call at the outset. For example, "I wanted to set up a date to discuss our marketing plan with you." Then ask, "Can you spare XX minutes to talk about that?" By stating the reason for your call and then asking for a specific amount of the person's time, you'll put yourself at a business advantage. People will enjoy hearing from *you* more than from those callers who simply assume they have time to talk about "whatever."

Tip #39

Keep your cool
with telemarketers.

That telemarketer won't take no for an answer. (Let's face it, the person is *paid* not to take no for an answer.) Instead of engaging in a battle of words or trying to see who can interrupt whom more dramatically, wait for the next question and respond to it by saying, "I'd like to speak to your supervisor, please."

Once you've made this request, most phone reps will realize that they're obligated to put you through to the manager. When you reach the person's superior, calmly and tactfully explain that you don't want to be called again. For example:

> *"Hi, this is Joan Bennett. Your sales rep called me at 508-555-1212. I'd like you to delete my name from your call list, because we don't accept unsolicited calls at this number. Would it be possible for you to take care of this for me this morning/ afternoon/evening? Thank you."*

Tip #40

What to do and what not to do when meeting over the phone.

When talking to another person for the first time by phone, drop the person a note following the call. This will let him or her know that you are one who follows through and goes that extra mile. If you're lucky, this gesture will lay the foundation for a strong new business relationship.

Whatever you do, refrain from "jumping the gun" by asking the person to send you a business card by mail. A business card is a "signature"—coming out and asking for it is more than a little uncouth. Even if he or she would have forgotten to send a business card, you may seem tacky for having asked. If you need the spelling of a person's name or to confirm the office address, ask for it during the conversation.

Tip #41

Keep the customer
satisfied over the phone.

Customer service begins with the first person who answers the phone!

If you are a telemarketer or a front-line person, such as a receptionist, secretary, or customer service rep, and you have to handle multiple calls on a daily basis, there's a one-word rule to keep in mind for all of your phone work: Enunciate!

It is disconcerting to any caller to hear a voice that skips along rapidly without pronouncing words properly. Mumbling conveys a poor first impression. To avoid sounding like someone who just wants to get off the phone as quickly as possible, take care to slow yourself down. Try adapting your rate of speech to that of the caller.

After all, which greeting would you rather hear when you contact someone:

"Sagreatdayatabeeseecorphowcanihepyasmornin'?"

Or:

"It's a great day at ABC Corporation! How can I help you this morning?"

Also, if you work at a reception desk or handle any kind of incoming call, avoid making callers feel like they're getting the bum's rush!

Be patient with both the caller and yourself. Pause after asking a question, in order to give the caller time to respond.

Refrain from breaking in with your own suggestions after a fraction of a second.

And be honest. If you have other people on hold, let the caller know this and ask for his or her cooperation. Then get back to the call as quickly as possible. Be sure to thank the person for holding. Remember: However patient a caller may be, nobody likes to be kept waiting for too long.

Tip #42
Smile your way
through multiple calls.

Handling a lot of calls? Smile as you do so.

Anyone who fields multiple calls in any capacity should post a sign over his or her desk reading, "Say It With Smiles!" This dictum is especially true for telemarketers, who suffer serious disadvantages when matched against representatives who hold meetings or sell products in person. Where others are able to use body language and visual aids to make their point, you have to rely solely on the tone of your voice. You must grab and hold the attention of those you are calling if you want to make a sale. A voice that sounds bored and disinterested, or someone reading a script with nothing more than a drone, may only "turn off" a potential customer.

So practice your smiling. Even though the person on the other end of the line cannot see your face, a positive attitude can be conveyed by your intonation, and customers will respond to that in kind. If you're having difficulty remembering to smile, then keep a mirror at your work station and check yourself as you talk, to ensure that your lips are curved upwards.

Along with a smile goes simple, basic courtesy. Remember that telemarketing calls can frequently be disruptive to those you are calling, so be sensitive to this. Many sales trainers advocate a sensitive, attentive telemarketing style, rather than the annoying rat-a-tat strategy that guides so many of the calls we receive. This book is not a sales guide, of course, however you should know that most individuals react with strongly negative emotions to telemarketing appeals of the "You are interested in saving money, aren't you?" variety.

My advice: Avoid launching into your sales pitch the minute the potential customer picks up the phone. Be polite, state the caller's name, express your thanks for the person's decision to take the call, and ask for permission to proceed. It might sound something like this:

"Dr. Smith, thank you for taking my call. I'm calling about...Do you have a minute?" You may find that this simple, courteous question—delivered with genuineness and warmth—is received with appreciation and, therefore, gains you the attention you need to make your pitch.

Tip #43
Show understanding to tough callers.

"This is the third time I've called!"

"I want an answer immediately!"

"Repeat what I said? What are you, deaf?"

Observing proper telephone etiquette can be difficult when there is a particularly troublesome caller on the other end of the line. If your job involves fielding calls all day, your nerves can often be worn to a frazzle from your interactions with such callers. Resentment is inevitable when callers take their own anger and frustration out on you and fail to recognize that you are only an intermediary.

Unfortunately, this is part of your job. You simply can't avoid the impatient, difficult types who will expect answers you can't provide and make impossible demands of you. The trick to handling them is to invoke a variation of the Golden Rule: "Do unto a caller as you would have a caller do unto you."

Put yourself in that caller's place. You're phoning a company expecting to talk to a certain person or to get an answer to a particular question. Instead, you reach someone who not only doesn't know what your contact's schedule is, but is in no position to answer your question and doesn't know to whom your call should be transferred. All you can do is leave a message and wait (indefinitely) for your call to be returned. Wouldn't you feel a bit frustrated?

Granted, you are not paid to be a sounding board for frustrated callers with poor manners. But as the person who has picked up the phone, you are the company's representative and the one who is going to provide a crucial impression of the type of people your company employs. Therefore, it is up to you to display good manners and a willingness to help. A true professional is eager to go the extra mile to put callers at ease. This means employing good listening skills, conveying detailed messages, and doing whatever it takes to ensure that questions are forwarded to the proper individuals. You would, after all, expect no less than this when you are looking for assistance!

When callers recognize that you really are making a sincere effort to work with them, you'll be amazed at how quickly their attitude improves.

Courtesy begets courtesy!

Tip #44

Know when and how to ask the other party to call you back.

If you use the phone to transact a great deal of your business and find yourself with mounting phone bills as a result, it may be time to examine your telephone usage. In particular, if you are dealing with suppliers who are making money from your business, yet you are bearing the greater burden of the telephone costs, you need to rectify this. Any phone conversations that last longer than five minutes should be at the expense of the party who stands to profit most (or to be more precise, eventually gets paid) as a result of the call.

Suppliers of a product or service should recognize that it is their responsibility to assume the long-distance calls that may result in business for them. To ensure that this happens, request a callback when you place your initial call, being sure to specify a callback time. For example, "I will be in the office between 2 and 4 this afternoon."

There are other approaches, of course. Countless companies have installed 800 numbers for their customers' convenience. Still others will back up these techniques by providing you with a toll-free facsimile number when facts and figures or special messages need to be communicated. But if the company you're dealing with has not yet changed to a more cost-effective system, then you should tactfully yet firmly ask your contact to return your call and spare you a long-distance charge. For example, you may say, "Jim, I'm afraid this call's going longer than our accounting department would like. May I ask you to call me back this afternoon between 1 and 3?"

Tip #45
Use Caller ID properly.

File it under "Intimidating Experiences of the Modern World": You place a call, you're listening to the phone ring, then the person on the other end of the line picks up the phone and, before you can say a word, addresses you by name, explains that he has to run off to a meeting, and asks when you're going to have those reports you promised to deliver.

New technology can be both a blessing and a curse. Caller ID, which was devised to help screen phone calls, is subjected to frequent abuse by its users and can create confusion for those who are calling when they are greeted before having had the chance to identify themselves. This is not just disconcerting, it's rude!

Proper Caller ID etiquette means that you use the device to prepare for a call by identifying its source. It is not meant to be a game of "one-upmanship," which can, in fact, backfire when the caller on the other end of the line does not coincide with the screen name you have for the incoming phone number.

Thus, two potential problems exist when Caller ID is misused: 1) The caller may be thrown off guard when he or she is addressed by name at the outset, and 2) the caller and the screen name may not be the same person, thus getting a telephone call off to an inauspicious start. To avoid confusion and to demonstrate your professionalism, answer the telephone properly! Use Caller ID only as a means to screen and prepare for calls—rather than as a means of showing off your new high-tech gadgetry. When you reach for the telephone, bear in mind that it is a tool, not a toy!

Key point summary

- Make sure you ask before you put the caller on speakerphone.

- Follow correct procedures when setting up conference calls; make sure someone is in charge of setting dates, verifying participation, and ironing out any kinks that may arise.

- Let the people who field calls for you know what you're doing.

- Know—and plan to avoid—the most common missteps committed on the phone.

- Avoid abusing the patience of fellow travelers when making calls on the road or in the air.

- Keep away from beepers that "sound off." They're annoying.

- Avoid excessive personal calls while you're on the job.

- Develop a personalized, direct, and professional greeting for your voice mailbox.

- Know when *not* to answer the phone.

- Make a point of checking voice-mail and e-mail regularly.

- Leave enough information in your phone messages.

- Don't ramble on while leaving a message in someone's voice mailbox.

- When you reach someone directly, explain why you're calling.

- Avoid pointless conflicts with telemarketers. If you don't want to hear from this company again, ask to speak with the manager.

- Follow up in writing when appropriate, and don't ask for business cards over the phone.

- Dealing with customers? Speak slowly enough to be understood, and pace your remarks to the conversational speed of the other person.

- Handling a lot of calls? Smile as you do so.

- Let tough callers know you understand.

- Understand when, and how, you should ask for a call back.

- Avoid playing "games" with Caller ID—it's rude and unprofessional.

Chapter 5

Cubicle Protocol and Time Management: Functioning Well in the Office

"As a man is, so he sees."
—William Blake

What do we see when we show up at work each day? A collection of deadlines? A pile of memos on a desk? A series of commitments in frantic pursuit of a finite number of hours? Or perhaps—just perhaps—the opportunity to interact harmoniously with those people with whom we share the workplace?

In the hectic world in which we live, we must manage both our relationships with co-workers and our own time if we are going to keep our interactions harmonious and our work flowing smoothly. In this chapter, you'll get some essential advice on co-existing with those people who have such a huge potential impact on your quality of life, those people with whom you probably spend half of your waking hours—your co-workers. You'll also get some important pointers on controlling your own schedule, rather than letting it control you.

Tip #46
Obey The 12 Commandments of Cubicle Etiquette.

Working in a cubicle can be a challenge! Aside from space limitations, the greatest common complaint that cubicle workers have is the invisible sign that hangs over the area proclaiming, "No Privacy Allowed." There are distractions galore in the modern workplace: typewriters, calculators, computers, and printers clicking, clattering, and humming away in adjacent cubicles; the personal conversations going on in the next pod that you can't help but overhear; and worst of all, the assumption of other cubicle mates that they can walk into your workspace whenever they like, without being invited or welcomed. A protocol can and should be established to help ease the situation for all those who must share a common area in the office. The following list suggests basic cubicle protocol for the modern workplace.

The 12 Commandments of Cubicle Etiquette

1. Thou shalt not enter another person's cubicle unless you are invited. (Recognize that an invisible door exists.)

2. Thou shalt not interrupt someone who is on the telephone by using sign language or any other means of communication.

3. Thou shalt think twice before interrupting someone who appears deep in thought. (When you must interrupt a person who appears to be deep in thought, say, "Excuse me. Do you have a minute for me?")

4. Thou shalt be aware of how your voice projects (if you laugh loudly, for example, ask yourself if others can hear you and how it affects their concentration).

5. Thou shalt realize that speaker phones and cubicles don't mix.

6. Thou shalt not discuss a confidential matter in a cubicle setting.

7. Thou shalt realize that everything you say makes an impression on your "internal customers."

8. Thou shalt not make or receive personal telephone calls during the workday except during breaks or lunch.

9. Thou shalt not establish eye contact with someone when you would prefer not to be interrupted (i.e., when you're on the phone or meeting with another person).

10. Thou shalt stand up and walk toward the entrance of your cubicle when you would like to keep an impromptu meeting short.

11. Thou shalt keep snacking to a minimum. (Your cubicle should not look or smell like a mini-cafeteria.)

12. Thou shalt recognize that your cubicle is a reflection of you. Keep it neat and orderly.

Tip #47

Send the right message to cubicle lurkers.

As though an open work area weren't formidable enough already, you've often got the challenge of a colleague who hovers around your cubicle, waiting for you to return, eager to separate you from the pressing project you need to work on. Usually, these folks are easy to recognize. They're the ones who want to discuss social plans, petty gripes with colleagues or family members, or other nonessential problems—usually when you're on deadline.

What to do? Acknowledge the person with a pleasant smile as you enter your cubicle, but stride purposefully to your desk. Don't initiate a conversation. If you do, the lurker may just follow you in (and perhaps never leave). Start working—perhaps by making a phone call—and hope the person has the presence of mind to realize that you're busy dealing with a critical project. If push comes to shove and the person insists on talking about nonwork-related matters, ask tactfully yet firmly to reschedule the meeting until after work hours: "Jane, I'd love to talk to you about the wedding shower for Patricia, however I've got a report due at 2 this afternoon, and I'm wondering if we can catch up on this after work, say at 5:30 today?"

Tip #48

Rework the "Do Not Disturb" sign.

Employees who work in cubicles or "pods" should set parameters for when they are available to other co-workers.

When you are not available, you could post a red paper sign outside the work area that reads, for instance, "Co-worker alert! I'm working under a project deadline until 11 a.m., but I want to hear from you. Please leave a note in my mailbox and I will respond to you by the end of the day today." When you *are* available, hang a green sign outside your area advising your co-workers that you're free for discussions.

Warning: This works well only if you alternate the signs frequently and give clear indications of when you will be available. Also, make it clear that your message applies to co-workers, not to superiors!

Tip #49

Keep cubicle decoration in balance.

Your cubicle is your home away from home...kind of.

If you're like most people, you'll spend more of your waking hours at work than you will at home, so the instinct to make your cubicle or other office space feel homey is understandable. But how homey is *too* homey?

Here's a rule of thumb that will help you make sure your workspace keeps everyone, including superiors and important outsiders, happy: Take a good, long look around your office. Then ask yourself, "Whose level would I like to be working at a year from now and what does that person's workspace look like? How audacious is the design? How many, and how obvious, are the personal items in that person's area?"

Follow the design lead of the person who's successful in the area you'd most like to call your own, and you usually can't go wrong.

Tip #50

Deal positively with a chronic complainer.

No matter where you work or what type of business you are in, it is impossible to avoid people who (it seems) live to complain. Complainers go with the territory in any job, and they often generate a feeling of negativity that can bring down morale for everyone. This in turn brings on resentment and ill feelings between co-workers and strains office relationships. It is best for all concerned to keep complainers in check as much as possible, but how do you keep from sinking to their level and lashing out with complaints of your own? ("It really drives me crazy when you complain about the cleanup schedule. Why do you have to dooooo that? It hurts my heeeead!") Here are a few tips that will help you institute solutions and keep new problems from arising:

- Listen to the complaints, rather than fighting them instinctively. Constant complainers usually continue because they feel no one is listening. Use active listening. It will provide an outlet for them that may result in an easy solution to the problem.

- Ask questions. Quiz the complainer closely on the problem and ask what he or she wants done about it.

- Be direct. Rather than misleading the complainer with promises you can't keep, be honest about what you can or can't do to help resolve the problem. You will do both yourself and the complainer a favor when you "tell it like it is."

- Recommend an assignment. Try getting the complainer to do something constructive towards resolving the problem on his or her own that doesn't require your intervention.

- Think before you agree. Even if you believe the gripe is valid, don't be in a rush to join the chorus. Maintain an attitude of impartiality, especially if other employees are involved in or affected by the complaint in question.

- Silence may not be golden. Saying nothing may imply agreement, which could compound the problem later. If you disagree, say so tactfully.

- Avoid contradictions. Complainers can weigh you down with all sorts of "Yes, but..." sentences when you are proposing solutions to the problem. Many prefer to gripe rather than to take action. Some will be quick to point out the contradictions in your ideas. Be consistent in your message and you'll help them avoid getting sidetracked by fresh (and fascinating) new horizons of inconsistency.

- Act as an example. Complainers need to be shown that there are ways of dealing with problems other than constant griping. Your example can be an effective way of getting a complainer to modify his or her communication style, rather than simply griping.

The best way to handle complainers is to encourage them to become proactive. Give them the attention they are seeking and guide them towards constructive solutions. You will help both them and the office as a whole.

Tip #51

Learn to manage your time.

Time management is an essential ingredient in business etiquette. Besides demonstrating how well you are organized and can handle mounds of work, it can also have an effect on your relations with business colleagues and clients. Nobody wants to have his or her time wasted by someone who is always arriving late at meetings or hasn't been able to complete a project by the assigned deadline. Sometimes, of course, circumstances prevent us from getting there on time or meeting that deadline; time management gaffes do occur quite legitimately. However, those who appear to make a habit of such gaffes are committing the sin of wasting precious time, not only for others but for themselves. In the business world, especially, time is money!

We all know that it is not always possible to meet a deadline that has been imposed on a task or project. This happens frequently in the business world. The important thing is not to make a habit of missing key deadlines. When you are consistently unable to complete a project on time, that says something about your ability to organize and manage your workload. However, on those occasions when a delay is inevitable, you should advise all concerned parties in writing of the time delay and the reasons for it. You should then come up with an alternative and reasonable deadline—and brook no further delays! One strike will not penalize you; two strikes will have people questioning your abilities; three or more strikes and you may be out of a job!

To avoid getting yourself into such difficult situations, try following these guidelines for managing your time:

1. Use only one calendar. Map out where you will be, what you are to do, what the relevant deadlines are, etc., on a single calendar. By keeping one schedule with you at all times, you will be more efficient—and you will save time because you won't be shuffling between six different planners.

2. Plan your work and then work your plan! That is to say, write it all down. Have a "road map" in front of you, with your strategy for the day worked out. Rather than piddling your day away deciding what to do first, you will actually be *doing* it. By setting up a schedule and sticking to it, rather than improvising your way through the day, you can post some dramatic time improvements. You may accomplish as much as 20 to 30 percent more each day. (These are the improvements people I've worked with in one setting or another have been able to post.)

3. Set realistic deadlines. Be fair to yourself! Sometimes a project that you promise to have completed by Tuesday may not need to be finished until Wednesday. Be realistic when you lay out your goals.

4. Put off until tomorrow what you really don't have to do today. In other words, establish priorities and tackle the most important tasks first. If you spend three hours "returning calls" to people who don't have anything to do with the accomplishment of major goals, there's a problem somewhere.

5. Make your voice mail work for you. When you are on a deadline, use voice mail to minimize interruptions from ringing phones. Callers would prefer talking to you when they have your undivided attention. Be sure to indicate in your message when you will be available to return their calls.

6. Touch a piece of paper once. Try following the "do it now" principle. If you don't need it, pitch it. If you are going to need it, file it. If you need to act on it, do so *now*!

By planning ahead in this way, you'll ensure timeliness in all areas—and leave your colleagues and business associates impressed with the way you do business.

Tip #52
Move beyond deadlines.

A deadline should mean more than the due date of a project. Before committing to a deadline, consider what it means to your schedule. If everyone in your workplace followed the rule, "The Proper Time To Do Something Is Before It Needs To Be Done," no one would ever be late with or for anything. In addition, we all might feel less frazzled, have more time, and many egos would be spared. If you haven't already found a way to be in control of deadlines and your time—rather than letting them control you— here are some ideas to keep in mind:

- The secret to never being late for an appointment or sending something later than you've promised is to commit to take action at an appropriate point *before* the deadline. Write down when the promised item needs to leave your hands in order for it to be received on time, and put that appointment date on your calendar.

- For an appointment, rather than focusing on the time you have to *be* at your destination, write down or commit to the time that you have to leave in order to get there, say, five to 10 minutes early.

- Underpromise and overdeliver. Try to build in a "buffer" that allows you enough time to resolve last-minute problems.

Delivering materials on time and showing up on time will help you shine professionally. So use deadlines and start times as beginning points, rather than as calendar entries.

Tip #53
Don't let others exploit your time.

Another crucial aspect of time management involves not allowing others to cut into your valuable time and keep you from finishing a project (or simply working in peace). While most people won't waste others' time intentionally, they may do it anyway as a result of their communication style. Here are a few tips for preventing such people from exploiting your time and for helping them to use their time more effectively:

- Assist people in getting to the point. Ask them open-ended questions, rather than closed-ended ones. "How did you arrive at that figure? What does it mean?" may leave your contact feeling less frustrated and more inclined to sum up quickly than "Did you double-check those figures?"

- If you can, let your body language do the work for you. When someone enters your office uninvited and you sense a possible breach of your time, you may want to convey the impression that you cannot or should not be disturbed. If you are at your desk, avoid eye contact. Keep writing or working on your computer. This will discourage people from initiating a conversation if they see you are doing something else. (When you really don't want to be disturbed, of course, the best solution is to close your door—assuming you have one!)

- When scheduling get-togethers, rather than saying, "Let's meet at 2 p.m.," specify beginning and ending times for one-on-one conferences: "Let's go over those figures between 3 and 3:15 today." Pleasantly and firmly let people know when you are available—and let them know when your time is up in just the same way.

Tip #54

Get out from under the clutter!

Do you really want to keep your hottest client waiting while you track down those specifications?

Americans waste a significant amount of time each day looking for lost and misplaced items. Studies have confirmed that the average U.S. executive loses six weeks per year retrieving misplaced information from messy desks and files. The more stuff you stuff away, the harder it is to find what someone else needs.

Estimates from various research organizations indicate that:

- 80 percent of all papers that are filed are never referred to again.

- Paperwork has been voted the biggest burden for small businesses.

- About 85 percent of accumulated clutter is the result of disorganization, not lack of space.

Rather than keeping a piece of paper because you "might need it," ask yourself, "What is the probability that I will need this piece of paper? Can I replace it? Does someone else have a copy? What's the worst thing that would happen if I didn't have it?"

Here are more questions to ask yourself before you decide to keep a piece of paper or throw it away:

- Am I keeping it "just in case," yet can't come up with a specific reason for holding on to it?

- Do I feel as though I should keep it because of who gave it to me or how nice or official it looks?

- Can I clearly envision and verbalize how I will use it again?

- Have I referred to this piece of paper within the last six months?

- Do I need it for legal or tax purposes?

- Do I have duplicates of it?

- Has it already been saved on a computer disk?

- Is the only reason for saving this sheet of paper that I've "always done it that way"?

Your office's appearance and your ability to handle the flow and filing of the paper that passes through it reflects strongly on you as an organized individual. When you get out from under the clutter, you regain control of your time and your space. Unclutter your office, and you will unclutter your life!

Tip #55

An organized briefcase is vital to your image.

Just as a well-organized office reflects your ability to manage your time effectively, so does a well-organized briefcase. By merely throwing papers into your briefcase without making any attempt to put them in order, you run the risk of looking foolish later when you have to hastily sort through them to find what you want or need. This wastes both your time and that of the executive who is impatiently waiting for an answer to his or her question.

Key point summary

- Familiarize yourself with The 12 Commandments of Cubicle Etiquette.

- Remember: The proper time to do something is before it needs to be done.

- Use intelligent guidelines for managing your own time. You should be especially careful to establish priorities and tackle the most important tasks first.

- Keep people from exploiting your time, and whenever you can, help them to use their own time more effectively.

- Take control of the paper that crosses your desk and ask yourself, "What's the worst thing that could happen if I throw this away?"

- Keep your briefcase neat and well-organized.

- Consider developing and posting a "co-worker alert" sign that notifies team members about when you are—and aren't—available.

- Handle cubicle workers tactfully yet firmly.

- When decorating your cubicle, follow the design lead of the person who's successful in the area you'd most like to call your own.

- Handle chronic complainers effectively: Listen to them and then encourage them to become proactive by guiding them toward constructive solutions.

Chapter 6

Meetings: Getting It All Together

*"Everything happens to everybody sooner or later if
there is time enough."*
—George Bernard Shaw

The problem with Shaw's observation, of course, is that
there frequently isn't time enough. Problems that need to
be resolved in short order require the input and experience
of more than one person. What to do? Hold a condensed-
experience get-together, one where you can take advantage of what everyone knows. To use the more popular
terminology, you call a meeting. (It beats waiting until you
know everything, right?)

Some people complain that they spend far too much
time in meetings. Others feel that group-based business
gatherings are the very best tool for avoiding major organizational mistakes, and are thus worth the time and effort
necessary to plan and participate in them. Whether you
fall into one of these two camps automatically or are

ambivalent about formal workplace gatherings, you'll want to know how to get the most out of the time you spend in meetings—and how to keep little problems from escalating into big ones with co-workers and superiors.

Once you follow the advice here on developing promptness, improving communication, and handling challenges, you'll be ready to take advantage of what you learned during the gatherings and put it to practical use.

Tip #56

Never arrive too early for a meeting.

Many people don't consider that arriving in someone's office more than five to 10 minutes before a meeting's scheduled time is a breach of privacy. Most of us are susceptible to tight schedules and to the "wrap-up-as-much-as-possible-before-the-powwow" syndrome that accompanies full days. Early arrival can definitely be an etiquette no-no. How would you feel if someone were sitting across from your desk, staring at you while you tried to make the most of the scant time remaining for some daunting task on your lengthy to-do list?

Although arriving early at an in-house meeting is usually considered positive, remember that in this case, "early" means no more than, say, three to five minutes before the scheduled start time. Even while following that guideline, you may well run into a situation where a colleague or superior would prefer that you take a trip to the water cooler while he or she uses those precious minutes to attend to some last-minute detail or other. Don't make the person ask you to leave. Be considerate. Discreetly step out until the exact meeting time arrives.

Making a habit of showing up early—and first—to every meeting can have a potential negative impact on your career: Your colleagues and/or supervisor may conclude that you have too much time on your hands.

Punctuality and promptness are certainly values to be honored, however, avoid letting your commitment to them blind you to the unintentional messages you may be sending by arriving too early, too often.

Tip #57
Know what to do when you're going to be late.

When being late to a meeting is unavoidable, it is important to cover yourself and demonstrate courtesy and consideration towards others. Say, for instance, that you are on your way to a meeting and have hit a traffic jam that clearly will delay you by anywhere from five to 20 minutes. If you have a mobile phone, you can and should call ahead to convey the problem and to allow the person(s) waiting for you to decide whether they should continue to wait or to cancel the meeting. If you don't have a mobile phone, look for the earliest opportunity to stop at a pay phone. If calling is simply impossible, then an apology and explanation upon your arrival will have to do.

Tip #58
Apologize when
you miss a meeting.

You are hard at work at your desk, when the telephone rings. It's your client, Mr. Big, and he has been waiting at the restaurant for the last 20 minutes—where are you? You check your calendar and gasp in horror. Your lunch meeting with Mr. Big is clearly noted, but you overlooked it! As you fumble for an excuse, you look at the clock and note that the restaurant is 30 minutes away from your office. Mr. Big (understandably) chooses not to wait further and cancels the meeting.

- *Rule number one:* Develop a routine that allows you to check your daily calendar the afternoon beforehand or first thing in the morning! Missing a meeting can have ill effects on your relationship with a client or a company superior. It is your personal responsibility to stay on top of your calendar. To this end, it is recommended that you confirm important business meetings a day in advance by phone or by e-mail. Let the person you are meeting with know that you will be doing this, and politely ask him or her to let you know if confirmation of the meeting has not occurred.

- When you do miss a meeting, apologize, rather than making excuses. You committed the gaffe and therefore you must be accountable for it. In the case of the Mr. Big scenario above, take the opportunity while you are on the phone with him to suggest an alternative plan. For instance, ask if you could meet him at his office with lunch in hand. If his schedule permits it, he may accept. If not, try to reschedule the lunch during the same conversation, or as soon as possible afterwards.

However much you apologize by telephone, *always* follow up with a written apology. Acknowledge your error and the effect that it has had on the other person's valuable time, and assure him or her that it will not happen again. Then make sure it doesn't!

Tip #59

Know what to say when colleagues go off on tangents.

Just about everyone would agree that time is the most precious commodity we have. So what should you do when a colleague goes off on a tangent—that is to say, insists on talking at length about something that isn't on the meeting agenda?

It is the responsibility of the person spearheading the meeting to acknowledge what is being said and to redirect the off-track participant. The goal is to get back to the meeting agenda.

If you're not the person who's running the meeting, you're probably at the mercy of whoever is. You may be able to raise a couple of tactful questions for the group as a whole—and by extension, the individual running the meeting—that explore the possibility that the topic raised may not be directly related to what's on the agenda. ("Did we want to wrap up X issue first?" or "Have we resolved Y yet?") Avoid dictating what should happen next. That's not your job. If your meeting is being conducted by someone who likes to "explore all the avenues," regardless of what's on the agenda, the sad truth is that your meeting may blaze a couple of uncharted paths.

If you are the person who's running the meeting, and if you feel there's some merit in the points your colleague just raised, you might say something like, "Let's give that topic equal time by getting it on the agenda for an upcoming meeting." You also might request that the person form a committee or work group for the express purpose of pursuing the topic in question—and be ready to discuss it at an upcoming meeting.

Tip #60

Handle attacks during the meeting with grace.

It seems as though there's a meeting attacker in every group. How do you let an overaggressive colleague know that he or she is being heard, but keep your cool and avoid attacking in return?

One way is to acknowledge what the attacker is saying and praise the positive intent behind what appears to be a negative outburst. ("Jane, it's very important to have someone who's as concerned about quality as you are. I'm grateful that you have insights to share on our department.") Where you can, acknowledge the valid points the other person has raised. ("I think there probably are some

areas where we can lower the reject level in the department.") Finally, shift the conversation into first person singular observations when you draw conclusions. ("I'll be
looking closely at this area over the next few weeks, however in the meantime, I recommend that we address the
point Charlie raised.")

One simple rule that can save your skin and keep your
blood pressure from boiling over: Stay away from aggressive "you" talk. When your attacker hears responses such
as, "You always," "You never," or "What you fail to realize
is," he or she has little choice but to escalate the conflict.

Tip #61
Navigate marathon
meetings with caution.

Let's face it, it's tough to get out of meetings that run
too long.

It's good etiquette to announce beginning and end
times for meetings. If you're running the meeting, making
scheduling announcements will (usually) be no problem. If
you're not running the meeting, then a tactful question or
two to the person in charge—well in advance of the meeting, if possible—will usually help you identify the ground
rules.

If you've been invited to a meeting that is running
more than five minutes beyond its predetermined schedule, you can try to excuse yourself discreetly, yet this is
sometimes easier said than done. If you can point to a
pressing commitment for which you must prepare, do so in

a positive, polite manner, and see how far you get on your way to the door.

When you can predict that a meeting will run for longer than scheduled, let the person who is running the meeting know before the meeting begins that you must leave at a certain time. Explain the nature of your commitment and then stake out a chair next to the door to make your exit an easy one.

Suppose none of that works and you're trapped in a meeting that simply refuses to stop? You'll need to do whatever you can to make it through the session "alive." If there are regularly scheduled breaks, take advantage of them. Stand up, stretch, walk around, visit the porcelain facilities. If you're consigned to a marathon meeting that has no scheduled breaks, suggest some! People function better when they are able to take breaks.

What you say might sound like this:

"Wow, an hour and a half! Jim, what do you say we break for 10 minutes? It may help us brainstorm better."

"While we're between topics, how would people feel about a quick intermission?"

"This is a critical problem and I know we want to tackle it while we're all at our best. We've been at this since four—may I suggest a break for dinner?"

Key point summary

- Remember that arriving more that five to 10 minutes early will likely be considered a breach of privacy.

- Can't help being late? Make a serious effort to phone ahead and let people know.

- When you do miss a meeting, make a point of apologizing forthrightly, rather than making excuses.

- Learn strategies for redirecting colleagues who go off on tangents during meetings.

- Become an expert at praising the positive intent of an abusive or attacking meeting companion.

- When you can predict that a meeting will run for longer than scheduled, let the person who is running the meeting know before the meeting begins.

Chapter 7

VIPs: Dealing With Key Decision~Makers

"All sins cast great shadows."
—Irish proverb

Even a minor error can have major implications, especially if the person who's affected by it is a big shot!

If you're like me, you know from personal experience that dealing with top officials can be a challenge. Lots of people are intimidated by the prospect of dealing with VIPs—by which I mean heads of corporations, government officials, visiting dignitaries, or key contacts within your own organization or one in which you hope to do business. But you can't let fear guide the relationship or you'll soon find that that "minor error" you were concerned about has turned into a series of major problems!

Not to worry, though. In this chapter, you'll learn how to handle encounters with people of high rank or status, maintain your poise, and come out looking great. Here's where you'll find advice on interacting with important officers, using your own words to best advantage, and establishing a good relationship with your boss. Once you've taken a look at the advice that follows, you may not completely rid yourself of all of those "butterflies in the stomach" that sometimes precede a meeting with an important decision-maker, but you should be able to approach these encounters with renewed confidence and composure.

Tip #62

When in doubt, ask questions.

When you're unsure about how to interact with an important decision-maker, your best bet is usually to ask nonthreatening questions in order to determine the best way to move forward. Rather than freezing up or trying to prove how smart you are, ask respectful, intelligent questions and see what happens next.

For example:

• "What are our department's main goals?"

• "What's the most important thing on the list for you?"

• "What sort of qualities are you looking for in a _____?"

• "How do you want me to proceed with so-and-so?"

Tip #63

Use the communication method your contact favors.

Looking for a good way to score points with the boss or anyone else whose opinion and respect you value? Mirror his or her favorite communication format!

Choose the way you are going to communicate with decision-makers and higher-ups based on the way they communicate with you. By doing so, you will be operating on their wavelength. For example, if your manager communicates with you via e-mail or fax the majority of the time, your responses to the person should be sent electronically or by fax. If your manager stops in to visit you when he or she has an update (or your client prefers to meet with you rather than talking about a topic via phone), emulate this behavior. Finally, if the person seems to communicate mostly by voice mail, make a habit of leaving voice-mail messages for him or her. The person you're connecting with will know that you're "on the right wavelength" the moment the message comes through.

Tip #64

Remember, you are your words!

One reliable rule for success when dealing with VIPs: Stay away from wishy-washy words when you're giving a presentation or making a speech. Stand behind what you say. As a rule, these folks hate double-talk and weasel language. They've been burned too many times not to.

I remember when I first learned this rule. Years ago, I was asked to give a presentation to a sales team. I gave what seemed to be a pretty sharp speech on the best ways to improve their face-to-face encounters with potential customers.

As I was leaving the room, I spotted the regional manager who had hired me. After thanking him for the opportunity to take part in the session, I said, "Please know that I am open to any suggestions from you about the best ways to improve." He took me up on my offer! He pulled me aside and told me, gently but firmly, that he hadn't hired me to tell his team what I "thought." I had been hired to make professional recommendations, and as such, should have been using words such as, "I recommend" or "I suggest," rather than, "It seems to me" or "I think."

From that day forward, the words "I think" have been removed from my vocabulary as a presenter and public speaker!

Tip #65

Learn how to get enough time with your boss.

Time is a valuable commodity, and it's frustrating when you can't get enough of it with your boss. Chances are that, even when you have a copy of his or her master schedule, a free moment you may be able to grab will be interrupted by someone else.

Unless yours is a quick question that can be answered in one or two minutes, it is better not to try to simply catch your boss in a free moment. Instead, jot your manager a note or send an e-mail asking when he or she can schedule 20 to 30 minutes of time to meet with you. By seeing your request in writing, your manager will recognize that the issue is probably important. You may even want to specify a certain date and time if you know your boss's master schedule.

Tip #66

Know what to do when a new boss comes on board.

You have the perfect boss, and you couldn't be happier with your job. Suddenly you learn that she has been promoted and a new manager is about to start. This means you now have to start from scratch in building up a good working relationship. This is likely to take some work, as the new boss has been hired from outside the company.

Along with a new boss comes a new department culture. Things change—like it or not. So rather than resisting the introduction of a new element into your department, welcome it. Accept the fact that the way some things are done presently will change over time and that it's possible it can be for the good of both the department and the company as a whole.

You are certain to gain the respect and support of your new boss if you respect and support him. Make it clear that you are there to assist him. Rather than offering unsolicited advice, wait to be asked before giving your perspective on matters. Give your new boss time to implement changes and to see how the changes work. Make yourself a valuable member of his team—work with him, not against him!

Key point summary

- Ask the right questions.

- Mirror the person's favorite communication format.

- Stay away from wishy-washy words when you're giving a presentation or making a speech.

- Dealing with a new boss? Accept it: Things are going to change. Avoid offering unsolicited advice, give the new person time to settle in, and keep an open mind.

- Use brief notes or e-mail to preschedule small chunks of time with your boss.

Chapter 8

Unfamiliar Settings: Handling Social Situations

*"Work is humanity's most natural form
of relaxation."*
—Dagobert Runes

Sometimes play *is* work—as when your organization expects you to "show the flag" at social gatherings. But mastering the principles for harmonious interaction at parties and other off-site gatherings can be a daunting challenge.

How can we be sure that the people we encounter during these "nonwork work" events showcase us at our very best? It may take a little practice, because our everyday instincts for proper behavior are usually divided into "business" and "social" spheres. When the spheres intersect, we may feel disoriented and have trouble responding quickly and effectively to challenges.

That's where this chapter comes in. It offers invaluable advice in areas that may not yet be "second nature" to you when you face work-related etiquette questions in social settings. By reviewing the ideas that follow, you'll help to make sure that you and your organization come across as polished and professional.

Tip #67

Set up a floor plan for social gatherings.

When entertaining guests at a business reception, make sure you have a crowd-control floor plan.

Position the "hosts" or key people within your organization in certain areas of the room so that guests can be waltzed from group to group in a smooth fashion. The most important person should be furthest away from the door. This will prevent people who want to speak with this person from crowding the entrance.

Tip #68

If you're planning a party, know when it stops.

When planning a business reception, be sure to limit it to two or three hours. This time frame keeps people from feeling worn out (especially when the reception takes place at the end of a business day). It also limits the amount of time that alcohol is served.

Tip #69

At receptions, silently repeat the mantra "who needs cliques?"

When you are involved in business receptions, avoid looking like you are part of your company or departmental "in-crowd." In other words, take the initiative—and show the organizational "flag"—by approaching people you don't know and taking the time and effort to become acquainted with them. Be sure that you ask more questions of others than you give information about yourself. If you notice that your employees or subordinates tend to cluster together in cliques rather than mixing with others, tactfully bring this to their attention. Clarify the reasons they are going to a certain business function, especially if it is for the purpose of networking. Explain what your expectations are and tell them that you will be meeting with them after the function for a "debriefing" session. Employees should be encouraged to sit next to people they don't know and to ask questions of others rather than talk about themselves, and to take responsibility for conversations with people on either side of them and to keep others involved in the basic flow of talk.

Tip #70

Make a point of handing out business cards.

It doesn't always take a formal meeting to bring business colleagues and customers together. Sometimes informal meetings and the chance to network can take place in the form of receptions, conferences, and organizational lunches. Take full advantage of such occasions. If a person appears interested in the service or product you represent, offer the person your business card. You just may get one in return!

Tip #71

Tactfully redirect "tech talk" at parties and receptions.

Perhaps you've had this experience: You hook up with a technical expert—someone who knows a certain computer system, World Wide Web browser, or transmission repair procedure inside and out. At a social gathering, this person goes off on a series of tangents that makes everyone else's eyes glaze over.

Try to keep the conversation accessible to everyone by smiling and saying, "That's a conversation in and of itself!" or "We certainly couldn't do justice to that subject tonight." Such "redirects" acknowledge your conversational partner's expertise and allow you to keep the discussion accessible to everyone.

Tip #72

Leave "shop talk" at work during nonwork-related gatherings.

Have you ever noticed that newcomers to a company sometimes seem to be the ones who have the hardest time letting go of work issues during after-hours gatherings?

Many new hires are recruited from out-of-town. The challenges of their jobs, when combined with the lack of a social network in a new city, can make establishing a personal sense of balance difficult for these folks. Their professional lives may consume most of their waking hours, and often the little time left at the end of the day is devoted to errands or other logistical matters. So they simply don't have much time to develop a group of friends outside of their work environment. The social and work worlds often fuse into one. If this weren't a recipe for burnout, there might not be a problem. But all too often, it is.

Help these folks out by setting an example of balanced living. Be true to yourself and your organization, which, after all, needs competent, creative workers, rather than overstressed automatons. Make a commitment: During evenings and weekends, your colleagues and you should find a way to talk about other topics—a televised golf tournament, a good new restaurant, a play you'd like to see.

Besides giving work talk a break, you will confirm to others that there really is life after work.

Tip #73

When eating out, don't "make like a cake."

At a business meal, when you've finished eating and the server asks whether you'd like your plate cleared, the appropriate response is a smile and a silent nod.

The inappropriate approach (whether or not a server is nearby) is to announce your status to the world at large by saying, "I'm done!"—making yourself sound like a cake that needs to be removed from an oven.

Tip #74

Synchronize your business meals.

Many businesspeople forget that the reason for breaking bread together is usually to interact with one another. Chowing down comes second! That means a "group approach" should prevail as the meal progresses.

How many times have you taken part in a business lunch or dinner and seen one person order an appetizer or dessert, without consulting the others at the table about what—or whether—they'd like to order? If you find that you're the only person at the table interested in a "peripheral" course, skip it! This is particularly important where appetizers are concerned. It's a major gaffe to make others wait for their courses to be served because you alone have chosen to explore the double-glazed chicken wings.

If you're the host or hostess, order peripheral menu items only if one or more of your guests does so. If you're a guest, order these courses only if others appear interested in doing so. The short rule is to listen and then order or don't order, based on what the others at the table are doing and/or what your host recommends.

Tip #75

Develop pasta consciousness.

If you are the guest of an Italian client whose roots are from Northern Italy, don't be surprised if you are not offered a spoon for securing those 12-inch strands of spaghetti on the fork. As a result of the French influence of cooking with white sauces, Northern Italians typically twirl without using a spoon. On the other hand, your clients whose roots are from Southern Italy may offer you a spoon and may use one themselves, because of the Spanish influence of using red sauces. This is just one of the countless areas of possible "culture clash" with overseas contacts. See the appendix for more advice on international etiquette.

Tip #76

Handle the "grace period" gracefully.

When hosting a dinner for clients in your home, you may request that they join you in your family's traditional words of thanks and prayer, although you should avoid making an issue of it. However, if you are hosting a meal in a restaurant or are a guest of someone else, avoid saying grace aloud. Simply say it to yourself quietly.

Tip #77

Follow your diet—quietly.

If you are on a special diet yet do not want to subject your client to explanations at the table, it is perfectly fine to call the restaurant ahead of time and request that the entrees be explained to you. Ask about what would be appropriate for your needs, based on the type of diet you are following.

Tip #78

Save those notes on utensil use for later.

If you notice that a colleague or subordinate is using the wrong utensil at a business meal, the best way to let him or her know this is by doing it right yourself. Your actions may raise the level of awareness of the person committing the *faux pas*. If this doesn't work, then take a moment the next day to talk to your co-worker about it. Be sure to use the "I" form instead of "you": "I learned that the appropriate utensil to use for the appetizer is the two-pronged fork to the right of the spoon," rather than "You used the wrong fork the other night and looked like a fool." By speaking in the first person singular, you will come across as providing constructive criticism, rather than being perceived as an attacker.

Tip #79

Give overseas visitors the VIP treatment.

When entertaining contacts from overseas or across the border, be sure to refer to them as "international" rather than "foreign." Frequently, the term "foreign" implies something undesirable, alien, out of place, or not belonging. When you are hosting a specific group from a particular country, you should, of course, incorporate it into your introduction ("our Chinese customers" or "our Greek clients").

It may seem like a small matter, especially when you consider that many of your visitors will be too polite to correct you, yet using insensitive terminology may offend your visitors and can cost you business.

Key point summary

- Develop a plan before you entertain guests at a business reception.

- Make a point of approaching people you don't know; take the time and make the effort to become acquainted with them.

- Know when to offer your business card at a reception or other business gathering.

- Try to introduce nonwork-related topics into the conversation.

- Avoid, at virtually all costs, announcing "I'm done!" when eating out.

- Keep your business meals in synch—make sure a "group approach" prevails when it comes to ordering appetizers, desserts, and such.

- Be prepared to eat pasta (or for that matter, anything) as your host's background dictates.

- Know when and how to suggest a moment of grace and thanksgiving before eating.

- Dieting? Call ahead and ask the restaurant what matches up with your current food restrictions.

- Use tact and discretion if you have advice to pass along to a co-worker on utensil use during meals.

- Entertaining people from other countries? Use the word "international" rather than "foreign" when it's introduction time.

Chapter 9

Off the Beaten Path: Coping With Challenges

*"The central problem of our age is how to act
decisively in the absence of certainty."*
—Bertrand Russell

Ours, of course, is not a world of certainty, and acting decisively within it can definitely be a challenge. Even so, some situations may appear to be considerably less certain than others—if only because we face those situations infrequently, and have not built up a series of habitual reactions for dealing with them.

Job interviews? Personal crises? Grooming emergencies? Questions about medication in the workplace? Announcements concerning pregnancies? These are not the types of problems that show up on our typical morning's to-do list. All the same, they are challenges that, despite their rarity, can be disastrous if mishandled. How, then, should we approach them?

134

In the following pages, you'll find advice for dealing with these and other unusual etiquette problems. By preparing yourself ahead of time, you'll stand a much better chance of responding appropriately when an unusual behavior question arises. On the other hand, if you rely on your "gut instincts" when faced with an off-the-beaten-path etiquette problem, you may come to regret your choice!

Tip #80

Avoid medicating yourself in front of a client or customer.

Sooner or later, most of us find it necessary to take medication for some health problem or other. It might be as simple as an allergy or as complex as a life-threatening illness. Diabetics may need insulin, while those with a chronic condition may have to take certain pills at certain times of the day.

Whatever the medication-related problem may be, it is best to avoid making a display of it in front of others, especially clients. After all, discussions of your health are likely to make others feel uncomfortable. Bear in mind that clients spend time with you to seek information or to gain your assistance. They are not meeting with you so that they can keep up with your health problems.

If the time to take your medication happens to coincide with the time of a meeting, you have several options. One is to take the medication either immediately before or after the meeting. If this is not possible, you should excuse yourself when there is an appropriate break in the conversation or meeting, and go to a discreet location—perhaps the bathroom—to take your medication in private.

Making a pill or injection the main thing a client (or anyone else) remembers from your meeting is a huge etiquette blunder!

Tip #81

Know when to schedule a close shave.

Not long ago, a reader of my column wrote me a letter asking: "Is it appropriate to shave at work or is it possible my manager or colleagues would see that as being a bit tacky if they walked in on me in the rest room?"

The best answer is that virtually anything is acceptable, if it's handled discreetly. If a man has a five o'clock shadow and would like to look as fresh for his 4 p.m. sales call as he did for his 8 a.m. strategy meeting, it's acceptable to take an electric razor to work. Rather than using it in the most high-traffic public rest room, however, he should choose one that's off the beaten path—or better yet, a private room. (He may also want to consult a cosmetologist for recommendations about daily facial care.)

A few more observations on facial hair are in order here. Rare is the company that would ban beards, mustaches, or sideburns. However, a man should take care that his facial hair is neat and presentable. Beards and mustaches should be kept trimmed, rather than assuming the long, scraggly, man-in-a-cave look. Sideburns should be mid-ear in length or shorter.

Tip #82

Handle the personal
crises of others sensitively.

Many people call our hotline about unprecedented situations. One of the thorniest of these is the question of how to show you care when someone in your professional life is involved in a personal crisis.

My recommendation is to emphasize the personal touch—without coming on too strong—and leave the other person in a position to determine what the next step ought to be. Rather than leaving a voice mail (too impersonal) or showing up at the person's doorstep unannounced (too forward), send the person a handwritten note. Let your acquaintance know that he or she and his or her family are in your thoughts at this time, and write that you're there to help if the need arises. This small gesture tells others that there is a real person to talk to, someone who cares and who is available to listen.

Tip #83

Treat hygiene problems with
discretion and understanding.

Talk about a touchy subject! One of your colleagues has a serious hygiene problem. We're not talking about minor mussed-hair issues or five o'clock shadow here, we're talking about persistent, impossible-to-ignore problems to which everyone, including important customers and potential clients, reacts negatively.

My recommendation: Approach the person on this issue only if you've established significant personal rapport with him or her. (If you aren't at this level, find someone who is, or talk to the person's supervisor.) Find a *private* setting where you can say something along the following lines: "As someone who has a great deal of respect for you, I'd like to share a sensitive story with you that someone brought to my attention about me a few years ago..." Then share a relevant incident from your own past. By focusing on yourself and allowing the other person to draw the obvious conclusion about his or her own situation, you'll be perceived as sharing, rather than as accusatory.

Tip #84

Keep the Tic-Tacs handy.

Say your company has a bagel club, consisting of 12 members. Each member of the club takes turns buying bagels on a rotation basis. Each member also has a choice of bagel flavors, but one person prefers onion and another one chooses garlic. You then must contend with "fragrant" breath for the rest of the day.

Another scenario: You are at lunch with some colleagues and someone orders a dish that is heavily laced with curry. You know that this person is scheduled to meet with an important client later in the day. Do you stop him from ordering a dish that will bear, shall we say, olfactory consequences and may well repel that big client?

Unfortunately, many people are unaware when their breath is affecting others and make poor decisions about the food they eat. After all, they can't smell it themselves, and unless someone speaks up and tells them, they will continue to indulge in these odorous foods. If the person is a colleague, someone you are close to, you may be brave enough to point out the trouble to them and discretely suggest that they make other choices. However, if the offender is someone you don't know all that well, you may try another, more subtle route. Try to carry a small supply of breath mints at all times. You may then offer one to the other person while in the act of taking one yourself. In this way you are taking discreet steps to at least temporarily resolve the problem. If the offender is even slightly astute, he or she will realize the providential nature of your offer of breath mints—and perhaps refrain from eating foods that provoke potentially career-threatening bouts of halitosis in the future.

Apply this same principle to your own eating habits. When making food choices, think about who you are with and (just as important) who you *will* be with. You won't want to walk into a big meeting reeking of garlic. Make wise food choices that take into account the people around you. If it's possible, take a trip to the bathroom to brush your teeth or rinse with mouthwash. And always keep the breath mints handy!

Tip #85

Make sure there's nothing to sneeze at.

Incredible as it may sound, there is a sneezing etiquette! Etiquette, after all, means "what to do and when." In the case of sneezing, this means always making a conscious effort to cover your mouth with your left hand when you feel a sneeze approaching. By doing so, you will have allowed your right hand to be germ-free when shaking hands or for offering an object to another person, assuming you're right-handed. (An interesting side note: If you interact with clients from the Middle East or India, you should know that they will especially appreciate that you have used your left hand to cover a sneeze. Both Middle Eastern and Indian etiquette dictates that you use only your right hand when offering something or taking something from someone else, and that the left hand be used for personal hygiene.)

Sneezing etiquette also dictates that you sneeze in a direction away from people. If this can't be done, then choose a direction where others are more than half an arm's-length distance away from you. If you are still too close, then at least face away from the people you are talking to, or isolate the sneeze so that it is in front of you.

The same principle usually holds true for coughing. Cough into your left hand and direct it away from people as much as possible.

Tip #86

Announce your pregnancy only after surveying the landscape.

Women may have a special bias to contend with when they become pregnant, especially if they are working in a company whose management is primarily or exclusively male. Rather than spreading the word immediately, take the time you need to develop a plan that will make sense for you within the context of your organization.

Eventually, of course, a pregnancy becomes hard to hide. Let your manager know before your new status becomes obvious and your style in clothes begins to change. For some women, that may be three to five months into the pregnancy.

It is important to be well-prepared when you inform your boss of your pregnancy. Know what you want! You should have a master plan prepared regarding how long you intend to continue working, the amount of time you intend to take off, when you plan on returning, and so forth. Also, familiarize yourself with your company's policy regarding maternity leaves, and talk to women who have been in the same situation. You may be able to learn some important pointers from these women about the organizational and mind-set obstacles you may face.

Tip #87
Handle "closet issues" with discretion.

There is, unfortunately, still a strong bias against homosexuals in our country. Although many would prefer that it be otherwise, it is usually best to keep your personal life personal, rather than advertising your sexual preferences in the workplace. If you work for a company with an open attitude about gays, so much the better. You may feel free to refer to your partner and bring him or her to business functions with you. However, if you are uncertain about what the corporate mentality may be or you feel the least bit uncomfortable with the effect your coming out of the closet may have on your co-workers, then it is probably best to attend company functions alone.

Tip #88
Make the right first impression at the job interview.

First impressions may never count more than when you are interviewing for a job. What the interviewer thinks of you upon the initial meeting can (and usually does) have an immense impact on the success or failure of your candidacy.

Here are some ideas to help get you through those all-important ice-breaking moments:

- Do your homework. Find out as much as you can about the company, its employees, the particular job you are applying for, and the person(s) with whom you will be interviewing. The more you know when you go into the interview, the greater the likelihood you will be called back for a second interview.

- Pay special attention to your grooming. Men's hair should be neatly trimmed and combed, and faces, as a rule, should be clean-shaven. (The exception: If you've done enough research on a company to ascertain that facial hair is acceptable— or even encouraged—within that particular organization, there's nothing wrong with appropriately groomed facial hair.) Women should adhere to the "less is more" rule in makeup, hairstyle, and fingernails. Unless you are applying for a position where flamboyance is allowed, nail polish should be kept to neutral tones.

- Dress appropriately for the position for which you are interviewing. For corporate positions, a neat business suit is best, with well-shined black or brown lace shoes or dress loafers. Women have more freedom in terms of color choices, but should still tend to more conservative tastes in dress. Avoid open-toed shoes or sandals. Instead, wear two- to three-inch pumps made of natural leather or suede, in a conservative color.

- Be sparing with fragrances. When in doubt, follow the "little dab'll do ya" approach—and remember, cologne or perfume should be applied only when you're getting dressed. Don't reapply it during a rest room break or just before going into the interview.

- Make sure your grooming and hygiene are impeccable. Be particularly careful about mouth odors. If you're a coffee drinker and you foresee that you'll have contact with individuals closer than an arm's length away, be sure to pop a breath mint into your mouth before the interview.

Tip #89

Let the interviewer know you're a star.

Once the job interview has begun, bear the following tips in mind.

- Stay positive! If you have had a bad experience with a supervisor in your past, find a way to praise that person's intent, and then talk about what you learned and how you grew as a result of working with him or her. If you can't say something positive, avoid saying anything at all! Instead of badmouthing a former employer, which may lead your interviewer to believe that you're a potential problem employee, focus on the future and keep your statements optimistic—no matter what.

• When it comes to salary specifics, remember, "He who speaks first about this topic loses." Your objective is to get the employer to bring up the matter of salary. When he or she does, consider asking, "Well, what's the best you can do?" Do your homework ahead of time—know how the employer's offer stacks up against similar offers.

• If you genuinely are interested in the position, show it by asking about the last person in the position, the short-term and long-term goals of the company, and the percentage of the time that new positions are filled from within the organization.

One final note on interview strategy:

Assertiveness is fine, however, avoid coming across as though you're taking over an interview. Recognize that you will have the upper hand during the interview (or during any meeting for that matter) if you ask as many questions as you answer. Rather than taking the risk of coming across as arrogant or self-absorbed, your aim should be to demonstrate that you are genuinely interested in what the interviewer is asking or sharing with you.

For more information on this topic, see the excellent book *Your First Interview, 3rd Edition,* by Ron Fry (Career Press, 1996).

Tip #90

Manage interest from potential employers wisely.

Sometimes *how* you go about your job search can adversely affect you and the people around you. Be careful— and courteous! Here are some guidelines that will help you through two of the most common and challenging situations:

Situation: You've been offered a job with one company and have an interview pending with another company for a position that interests you more. Is it acceptable to delay your decision on the first offer?

You bet! Such a situation can be used to your advantage in getting the best job at the best salary. When interviewing for the second position, let the interviewer know about the offer already received, and honestly, tactfully, and confidently outline what it would take for you to accept a different position (i.e., a higher salary or specific "perks"). Whatever is then offered to you, be sure to get it in writing. Think twice before accepting the first offer that comes along for fear that the second one won't come through. The fact is, you are a valuable asset to any company that hires you, and you should present yourself as such.

Situation: You currently are employed but are looking elsewhere. Is it acceptable for you to give potential employers your work phone number or pager number?

No. When you are on company time, 100 percent of your attention should be dedicated to your employer. When scheduling interviews or making follow-up calls, do so before or after work or off-site during lunch. This is not only the right thing to do, but it also displays your high code of ethics to individuals who may become your superiors in the future. By showing respect for your current employer's time, potential employers will know what sort of conscientious employee they will be getting.

Key point summary

- Remember that medicating yourself in front of a business contact can be a huge etiquette blunder. Either take the mediation before or after your meeting or excuse yourself when there is an appropriate break in the proceedings.

- Men: If you can find a low-traffic, private area, and you wish to shave discreetly in the afternoon to avoid a five-o'clock-shadow look, feel free to do so.

- When dealing with a colleague who is facing a personal crisis, emphasize the personal touch and let the other person decide what the next step should be.

- Don't approach a colleague about a hygiene problem unless you've established significant personal rapport with that person. If you do decide to address such issues face to face, do so in a private setting and establish yourself as the person's ally.

- Know when and how to share a breath mint with a colleague without giving offense.

- Cover your mouth with your left hand when you feel a sneeze approaching.

- Planning to announce your pregnancy? Work out a master plan beforehand; if possible, talk to women in your organization who have faced the same situation.

- If you are uncertain about your organization's attitudes, you may wish to keep sensitive personal information private.

- Make sure you leave the right first impression at a job interview. Be prepared and pay close attention to dress and grooming issues.

- Show poise, optimism, and intelligence during the job interview itself.

- Handle job-related inquiries from outside your organization with care; don't send the wrong signals to prospective or current employers.

Chapter 10

Common Questions

*"A handful of action is worth more than
a bushel of theory."*
—Anonymous

In this section, we'll take a look at some etiquette problems from the "front lines"—real, live readers of my weekly newspaper column who took the time to contact me about their own real, live etiquette problems at work. The answers to these questions will offer you insight into dealing with some of the more interesting variations on day-to-day business etiquette.

And, by the way, as I mentioned in the Introduction, if you have an etiquette question you'd like me to address, feel free to contact me! I realize that the advice offered in this book can't supply detailed responses to every possible business etiquette challenge you may face on the job. Let me know about the issues you're facing at work—and I'll do my best to find possible solutions.

Drop a line!

Tip #91

Help others keep industry jargon to a minimum.

Question: How can I encourage new acquaintances to be more sensitive about the use of insider jargon in social situations? The other day, I was at a professional organization meeting. Several of the people were talking about what was going on in their industry. It was difficult to get involved in the conversation because they all seemed to be speaking their own language—using acronyms that meant a lot to them and nothing to me and the other people at our table.

Answer: While some people may assume that everyone understands their particular abbreviations and industry jargon, others may actually perceive it as a "foreign language." The next time you find yourself in this type of situation, simply take the plunge and ask the people to assist you by clarifying what the acronyms mean. By requesting clarification, you may heighten their awareness and they may either ask if everyone knows what certain abbreviations or insider talk refers to or refrain from using exclusionary talk during gatherings that include "outsiders."

Tip #92

Attend to appropriate (female) bathroom issues.

Question: Some women just don't seem to get it! A company bathroom mirror should not be used for curling hair, plucking eyebrows, admiring oneself, or reapplying perfume. A company bathroom mirror is for freshening up, washing hands, and reapplying lipstick. Where do people get the idea that these actions aren't noticed by others who are also using the facility? Isn't this a breach of workplace etiquette?

Answer: Long-term monopolization of public facilities is a breach of etiquette, and don't let anyone tell you differently. Business and social manners dictate that you avoid excessive primping in public locations. That includes using perfume as though it were insecticide, taking over a sink when others may need the space, brushing or flossing teeth in a conspicuous location, etc. These matters should be attended to in a private area, rather than a frequently visited public bathroom.

Tip #93

Attend to appropriate (male) bathroom issues.

Question: Before I began working for my present company, I thought that all men were taught to respect the "one over rule" when using public rest rooms. In other words, when entering a rest room with three urinals, the first man should use either the first or the third urinal. The second man stepping up to a urinal should use the one that is one over—or two urinals away from the one being used. The only time the center urinal should be used is if it is the only vacant one. Some men seem to have skipped this lesson—and the one dictating that eyes should be kept straight ahead or down. Although this is a rather raw topic, I would be most appreciative if you would address it. Do the rules I mention still apply?

Answer: They certainly sound sensible enough. Everyone needs dignity and privacy. Our private space should be respected—even (perhaps especially) in a public bathroom. Until a better set of guidelines comes my way, I'll wholeheartedly endorse yours. You may have helped to educate a new generation of men on bathroom etiquette!

Tip #94

Be prepared for the "wandering eye."

Question: At a recent client conference, one of my best clients and I went to dinner. This person threw me for a loop when he expressed his interest in doing more with me than business. He expressed a romantic interest in me! (I'm engaged.)

How does one handle such a situation?

Answer: I hope that you let this person know that, although you value him as a client, you are already involved in a healthy personal relationship, and you don't believe in mixing business with personal matters. Setting limits gently but firmly is your best approach in this sensitive situation.

How does that old saying go? "You don't get your meat where you get your potatoes." That's a colorful way of saying that lots of things can go wrong when people put romance where it doesn't belong. You can jeopardize your career, start gossip, lose the trust of important higher-ups, cause political problems, or if one of you is married, earn the wrath of a wronged spouse.

One way to avoid being confronted with the awkward situation you describe is to arrange to have a minimum of three people in attendance at future dinner get-togethers. If you had done this, the unwelcome advance almost certainly would never have been made.

Tip #95
Don't send the wrong message at parties.

Question: I attend many company functions at which the spouses of my clients and colleagues are invited. One of my best clients actually chose to leave our firm and do business with a competitor because he perceived me as flirting with his spouse at our holiday gathering! (In fact, I wasn't flirting with anyone.) How could I have avoided this?

Answer: Natural, enthusiastic, outgoing behavior can be misconstrued as romantic interest in another person. The situation you describe is not at all uncommon. People at parties often try to throw the limelight on the persons they know the least well. This is a fine instinct, but in situations such as the one you describe, it's not a good idea to pay as much (or more) attention to a spouse when there's the potential for misinterpretation.

Tip #96

Save the love notes for after hours.

Question: Two unmarried colleagues in our office began a romance. On most fronts, they handled their personal relationship in a very discreet manner. However, they recently committed a *faux pas* that has made their relationship known to everyone in the company. One of them decided to woo and coo the other by sending a love note on the company e-mail system. The message was mistakenly transmitted to an entire address group! Any thoughts on how this could have been handled better?

Answer: Sure—save the company e-mail system for business use only. Unless you're looking forward to a dressing-down from the CEO, save the wooing and cooing for personal time. And remember, many e-mail systems keep track of every message sent, whether or not the message is regarded as confidential in nature. If you don't want Mr. or Ms. Bigshot reading the message, don't send it out on the company e-mail system.

Use business tools for business. Save love letters for after-hours!

Tip #97

Stand tall.

Question: When talking to someone who is confined to a wheelchair, is it appropriate to bend or kneel down to the person's level?

Answer: No. You shouldn't bend down to talk to a person who is confined to wheelchair, any more than you would stoop down to talk to someone who is shorter than you.

While we're on the subject, avoid talking in a demeaning or condescending manner to people who are confined to wheelchairs or who suffer any other disabilities. Physical limitations do not imply reduced mental capacity.

Tip #98

Be card smart.

Question: What, exactly, should I do when someone hands me his or her business card?

Answer: When receiving a business card, look at it for a few seconds. When appropriate, a complimentary word should be said about the person's title, logo, business card design, etc. The card should be placed either on a table where business is being conducted or in a planner or portfolio. A business card should not be placed in a wallet that is then put in your back pocket.

By the way, anyone who has business cards should not leave home (or the office) without them. Make sure the cards are clean and crisp, without even the slightest smudge or crease. Business contacts can be initiated, and cards exchanged, in some of the most unlikely places. Be prepared!

Tip #99

Give the big cheese the right kind of ride.

Question: How can I make the best impression when picking up a VIP at the airport?

Answer: For starters, make sure your car is immaculately clean—everywhere. Don't make the mistake one of the readers of my weekly newspaper column made. She was assigned to pick up her boss's boss at the airport. Recognizing that her car was an "extended office"—and a reflection of herself—she washed it inside and out. Then she made the *faux pas*: She threw everything from her backseat into the trunk. When it came time to pick up the big boss, it turned out the only place the oversized luggage would fit was (you guessed it) the trunk of the car. She was mortified. Let's just say this executive's impression about this lady's neatness wasn't as positive as it could have been. An unfinished car cleaning is not enough!

Tip #100

Learn how to work with receptionists.

Question: What is it with some receptionists? When I show up for appointments and give them my name, they inevitably ask, "What was your name again?" Shouldn't these front-line people be groomed to make better first impressions than that?

Answer: They probably should, however, bear in mind that the receptionist's job is a difficult and thankless one.

A good receptionist will write down both a caller's name and a visitor's name the moment it is said (even if an unconventional name means setting down a phonetic transcription). This strategy allows the receptionist to announce the caller/visitor to the person in the office. It also allows her to be in control of the situation by using the appropriate name.

One way to assist a receptionist in properly announcing you is to have your business card in hand when you approach the reception area. I can assure you that this gesture will be much appreciated by these individuals who must juggle telephone calls and visitors at the same time.

Tip #101

Navigate the "Miss"/"Mrs."/"Ms." problem.

Question: When a woman announces herself for an appointment, should she do so using her marital status? And while we're on the subject, what do I do when I'm introduced to a female client who is of the same generation as my mother? Should I use the person's first name if the person who introduced us is doing so, or should I refer to her by her last name? If I should use the last name, what do I put in front of it, "Mrs." or "Ms."?

Answer: The answer to the first question is a resounding no! It's tacky for a woman to refer to herself as "Mrs. Jane Smith," just as it would be inappropriate for a man to announce himself as "Mr. William Jones." Titles should be used by others, rather than by the person introducing or announcing himself or herself.

When meeting a client who is significantly older than you, address the person by his or her last name even if your colleague is on a first-name basis with the person. (In the situation you describe, you should use "Ms." before the last name unless you're instructed to do otherwise.) If the person wants you to address him or her using a first name, you will be told. Remember, you can never get into trouble for being too formal, but you can for being too informal.

Key point summary

- Help new acquaintances to be sensitive about the use of insider jargon in social situations; ask for clarification for the benefit of any outsiders who may be present.

- Brush up on (female) bathroom etiquette: Avoid monopolizing public spaces.

- Brush up on (male) bathroom etiquette: Follow the "one over" rule and respect the privacy of others.

- Be prepared to set limits gently but firmly when a business contact makes inappropriate romantic overtures.

- Be sure you're sending the right message at parties—focus on both spouses in attendance, not just one.

- Use business tools for business and save love letters for after-hours.

- There's no need to bend down to talk to a person who is confined to a wheelchair, any more than you would stoop down to talk to someone who is shorter than you.

- Know what to do when someone hands you a business card.

- Make the best possible impression when picking up a VIP at the airport—clean your car thoroughly, including the trunk

- Treat receptionists with respect and help them out by providing a business card when you approach the reception area.

- Use "Ms." before a woman's last name unless you're instructed to do otherwise.

Appendix

International Etiquette

When doing business in Australia

Greetings

Typical greetings are "Hello" and "G'day," rather than "Good morning" and "Good-bye."

Be prepared to offer your business cards. However, don't be surprised if you do not receive one in return.

Because Australia is a society that places less emphasis on formal social status than many other countries, titles are not used in introductions to gain respect. Actions and reputations generally outweigh titles.

Conversation

Be ready to establish rapport by making "small talk" before getting down to business. You will find that Australians tend to be direct and will often expect you to speak your mind.

Appropriate topics of conversation include sports and tours you have taken while in Australia. If you choose to discuss politics or religion, be ready to banter. Besides enjoying your strong opinion, bantering is also considered a form of entertainment.

Punctuality

Punctuality is both respected and a basic social norm. If you are late, this fact will reflect negatively on you and your organization.

Public manners

When riding in a taxi in Australia, you will be expected to sit in the front passenger seat rather than in the back seat.

A warning: The popular American "thumbs up" sign is considered to be an obscene gesture in Australia.

Business dress is generally conservative.

Business entertaining

If you are in a pub, it is appropriate to take a turn "shouting for a round" (that is, paying for a round of drinks).

When invited to a home, a gift, such as wine, candy, or flowers, is appropriate.

While dinner is served in the early evening hours between 6 p.m. and 8 p.m., a late evening meal called "supper" is taken a few hours after dinner.

When doing business in France

Greetings

When greeting a person who has earned the title of professor (*professeur*) or engineer (*ingenieur*), use the title in your greeting. These are considered marks of high accomplishment. Company managers and directors also are addressed by titles (i.e., "Monsieur le directeur").

Don't confuse someone who is addressed by the title "chef" for a person working in a kitchen; this term translates loosely as "boss."

Even after you have established a working relationship with a Frenchman, it will still be appropriate to maintain certain formalities (such as using last names).

Conversation

Good topics of conversation include where you are from, your interests, food, cultures of other countries, and sports.

Topics to avoid include how much things cost, what someone does for a living, prejudices about Americans, salary levels, and questions about a person's family.

Punctuality

Although individuals in southern France may be relatively relaxed about meeting times, it still is important to be respectful of your contact's time.

Public manners

While the French may stand closer to each other when talking than North Americans would, it is common to stand at an arm's length when discussing business.

Your hands should be visible at all times, including when you are seated at a table.

Business entertaining

It is considered acceptable to invite your French customer to lunch. If your French customer initiates the invitation, it is still in order for you to act as the host.

Although it is uncommon for alcoholic beverages to be consumed during lunch in the United States, this is very common in France. The French consider wine to be an aid to digestion and to act as a stimulant to the appetite.

The French, as their reputation holds, truly enjoy the art of dining. Just as many Americans "eat to live," the French seem to "live to eat." Business meals are not, as a rule, hurried meetings.

If you are invited to the home of a French associate and you bring flowers, be sure to take an odd number, and choose a flower other than chrysanthemums.

Business should be discussed only after dinner, when coffee (and perhaps brandy) are served.

Seating etiquette dictates that the host and hostess sit at the center of the table opposite each other. Guests are then seating in descending order of importance to the left and right.

You will not be offered a bread plate. When eating bread, you may place it on the table next to your main course plate.

When doing business in Germany

Greetings

When meeting people in a group, greet them and then shake hands with each person.

Rather than presenting your business card to your potential German customer, attach it to the material in your presentation folder. If you are involved in a meeting in which material will not be left, present your card upon leaving.

Be sure give a firm and hearty handshake.

It is common for a third party to introduce two people who do not yet know one another.

In southern Germany, and also in small towns, male professionals (lawyers, doctors, clergymen, etc.) should be addressed as "Herr Doktor." You will learn the person's last name when you are introduced.

When you are introduced to a woman, you will be introduced to her as "Frau" (Mrs.) or "Fraulein" (Miss) and the last name. If the woman works in a category considered to be professional, she should be addressed as "Frau (or Fraulein) Doktor."

Use last names unless you have been invited to do otherwise. During the transition from last-name basis to first-name basis, a drink ritual generally takes place. Your German friend will intertwine his right arm with yours, and with drinks in hand, will say, "To brotherhood." Return the toast.

When you say farewell to a group, address everyone in the room, beginning with the top-level person.

Conversation

Take note: The person who speaks the most softly in a meeting usually is the person who has the most authority.

Even if you are not fluent in German, "Guten tag" (equivalent to the English "Hello") should be part of your conversational repertoire. Similarly, "Danke" and "Bitte" ("Thank you" and "Please," respectively) should also be natural elements of your vocabulary.

Appropriate topics of conversation include hobbies, soccer, the places you've traveled in Germany, and the duration of your stay.

Topics to avoid include World War II and personal questions, such as, "How many people are in your family?"

Punctuality

Being prompt is of the utmost importance when interacting with Germans.

Public manners

It is considered impolite to put your hands in your pockets.

Gum chewing in public is also considered rude.

Germans may not use a smile as a nonverbal cue that they are pleased about something.

During a business meeting, expect the doors to be closed.

Be sure to walk to your contact's left. By doing so, you will be giving the person a position of respect.

Sit down only after you have been offered a seat.

Business entertaining

When inviting a German to eat with you, do so for lunch rather than for breakfast. If business is going to be discussed, do so prior to eating or after your last course.

Appropriate gifts include unwrapped flowers in a quantity other than 13. Your choice in flowers should be those other than lilies (which are reserved for funerals) or roses (which have a romantic connotation, regardless of their color).

When doing business in Hong Kong

Greetings

A handshake and slight nod of the head is considered appropriate when meeting a business contact.

Acknowledge the most senior person first by bowing.

If you know the title of the person, use it in the greeting. ("Mr. Yu," "Dr. Yu").

Be sure to have your business cards translated into Chinese on one side. Present your business card with both hands.

Conversation

Appropriate topics include how a person is feeling and a recent business deal.

Topics to avoid include politics, censorship, and protest movements.

Punctuality

Be sure to show your respect by being prompt. Punctuality is a much-appreciated virtue in Hong Kong.

Public manners

It is important to maintain a two arm's-length distance from your contact. Touching and patting are considered taboo.

Feet should be facing the ground rather than having the soles of shoes showing.

Business entertaining

Be prepared for an eight- to 12-course banquet. You may be involved in this type of meal after a business relationship has been established.

Be prepared to use chopsticks. When you are not using them, lay them on the rest or across the bowl—never place them vertically.

You may be offered a finger towel rather than a naplin at the end of a meal.

When eating rice, be sure to leave most of it in the bowl by the time the last course is concluded. Otherwise you will be perceived as not having had enough to eat during the meal.

Gift-giving is considered a business custom. Avoid giving a clock. This item is equated with death.

Just as with business cards, present a gift with both hands.

Open a gift in front of the person who gave it to you only when requested to do so.

When doing business in Indonesia

Greetings

Indonesian etiquette dictates that you shake hands the first time you meet a person, and not again. (The exception: Handshaking is also considered appropriate when someone is leaving or returning from a long trip.)

If a person touches his heart when meeting you for the first time, it means that the individual is very honored to meet you.

Titles (doctor, professor, and so on) are generally considered important and should be used in conversation.

It is wise to have your business card translated into Indonesian on the back of the card. You should present your card with both hands. When someone else presents a business card, make a point of studying it for a few seconds. When you choose to put away the card, be sure to put it in a card case or in your personal planner. Do not put the card in your wallet and slip it into your back pocket.

Conversation

Appropriate topics of conversation include family, food, the weather, and travel experiences. Although you may feel uncomfortable being asked personal questions about your own family, the cost of something you bought, and so on, it is acceptable to ask similar questions once they have been posed to you.

(If you are visiting Java, however, you should avoid topics such as family, purchases, and possessions.)

Punctuality

Promptness is appreciated.

Public manners

When you are in a private home or mosque, be sure to remove your shoes. Point them toward the door from which you entered.

Hugging and kissing in public is considered inappropriate.

Indonesians would, as a rule, rather be wrong than not be able to give you directions. For that reason, it's a good idea to ask a few people to confirm the directions you have been given.

If you are at a gathering in Java and are introduced to a group whose members all represent the same organization, it is not necessary to shake hands with each person.

Business entertaining

Rather than giving your Indonesian client a gift, consider passing along a compliment or thank you note.

Understand that it will be considered good manners to take a second helping of food. Recognize, too, that eating is regarded as a very private matter and that conversation will therefore be kept to a bare minimum.

It is considered good manners to leave a taste of food on the plate and a few sips of your beverage in the glass.

Eat with your right hand, rather than your left hand.

Be aware that women may be seated at separate tables from men. (In Java, however, men and women may be seated next to each other. The most important male guest will typically be seated next to the host, just as the most important female guest will be asked to sit next to the hostess.)

While a fork and large spoon will be available for you, a knife will not. Food is served in bite-sized pieces, so a knife will not be needed. Use the fork as a tool for putting food on the spoon.

When doing business in Japan

Greetings

When meeting a Japanese business contact, the bow is still the tradition. The deep, formal bow should be used for the initial greeting. To perform this bow, bend your body at about a 30-degree angle from the waist. This bow should be held for just a couple of seconds.

How low should you go?

With business subordinates: Allow them to bow longer and lower than you do.

With equals: Match bows, however, add an extra bow in situations where it is appropriate to pass along a note of respect (i.e., when bowing before someone who is older than you, a customer, or some other respected person who is technically "on your level").

With the person who is of a higher rank than you: You should out-bow this person. Keep your eyes respectfully lowered. If you know your contact outranks you, bow first and go low!

When you're unsure of status: Bow a shade lower than the other person.

For men: Palms should be face up, toward your knee.

For women: Hands should be folded in front of you as you bow.

Westerners may initiate a handshake after a bow.

Last names rather than first names always should be used.

Business card rules

1. Have your cards printed in English on one side and translated into Japanese on the other side.

2. Carry your cards at all times.

3. When presenting your card, be sure to have the writing facing the person receiving the card.

4. Present your card with two hands.

5. When handed a Japanese contact's business card, study it carefully. Keep the card out and place it on the table in front of you when you are seated. Do not put the card in your wallet and slip it into your back pocket.

6. You will be expected to exchange your card with just about everyone you meet. Have plenty of cards on hand.

Conversation

Topics to discuss include Japanese food, sports (such as baseball), Japan, other places you have visited.

Topics to avoid include your career, World War II, prices, your personal life.

Remember, "silence is a virtue"—especially in the Japanese culture. Rather than filling awkward moments with "small talk," recognize that to the Japanese, silence is equated with tranquillity.

Punctuality

Punctuality should be observed at all times. The Japanese culture is extremely time-sensitive.

Public manners

Even if you are experiencing displeasure or are upset about something, you should smile to show self-control.

Don't touch. "Backslapping" is likely to be seen as a major lapse in etiquette.

When you need to blow your nose, do so discreetly, preferably in private, with a paper tissue. Dispose of the tissue immediately. You don't want to be glimpsed putting a used tissue away in a pocket or purse; this is regarded as crude.

Bear in mind: To the Japanese, laughter can mean confusion rather than reacting to something funny.

Careful—the American "okay" sign means "money" in Japan.

Business entertaining

The reason for these get-togethers is for building friendships. Be prepared for a long meal. You may be entertained by karaoke or Sumo wrestling.

Consider it an honor when you are invited to a Japanese home. Be sure to remove your shoes at the front door; you will be offered a pair of slippers. Follow your host's lead if you're uncertain about when to remove your slippers and when to put them on.

Chopstick etiquette dictates that you place the sticks on the rest when you are not using them; don't leave them in your food. Whatever you do, avoid standing chopsticks straight up in the air or pointing them toward your hosts.

A box of fine candy is an appropriate gift to bring upon being invited to a Japanese home.

You may choose to give a more lasting gift (such as a pen and pencil set). If you do so, wrap it in pastel paper without a bow. Keep in mind that odd numbers are considered lucky.

When you are offered a gift, thank the person. Before taking it, wait for the person to offer it to you a few more times. As with business cards, accept a gift with both hands.

Drinking etiquette

Four ironclad rules:

1. Never pour your own drink.
2. Always lift your cup when someone is replenishing your drink.
3. Never let your guests' cups remain empty.
4. Take turns pouring for each other.

Drinking is a part of the socialization ritual in Japan; make it a time to cultivate friendships and trust. However, avoid getting too happy! (Many an American business person has regretted letting too much sake become a "truth serum" in social encounters with Japanese contacts.)

When doing business in Saudi Arabia

Greetings

Expect greetings to be very emotional . They consist of a "salaam alaykum" ("May God be with you"), followed by a handshake and then a "keef halak" ("How are you?"). If you already have a rapport with this person, you may receive a kiss on both cheeks. Your Saudi Arabian client also may take your hands in his as a way of saying, "It's good to see you."

Conversation

Topics to discuss include the country, the person's family (although not your contact's wife, as this may be misconstrued as a romantic interest), the countries where your Saudi client travels, etc.

Avoid discussing politics in any form. Do not discuss the social roles of Saudi Arabian women. Stay away from offering criticisms, even ones that seem insignificant.

Punctuality

Being on time is much appreciated.

Public manners

When reaching for something or offering something to a Saudi Arabian, be sure to do so with your right hand. Using the left hand is considered a taboo. When sitting, be sure the soles of your shoes face the ground. It is considered taboo for the soles to be showing.

Business entertaining

Realize the importance of accepting food and a beverage when offered. It is considered a personal insult to refuse what is offered.

Hard as it may be, don't show hesitation if you are offered sheep's eyes. These are regarded as a delicacy.

Alcoholic drinks should not be requested, although you may decide to accept if you are offered one.

Do not bring a gift to a Saudi Arabian's wife. (Again, this may be misinterpreted as a romantic gesture.)

When doing business in Singapore

Greetings

When greeting someone, use the person's title with the name. If you have not been told about a specific title, address the person using "Mr." or "Mrs."

Use a last name unless invited to do otherwise.

Do not ask to be addressed by your first name until you have been asked to address the person by his or her first name.

Present your business card with both hands.

Conversation

Appropriate topics of conversation include where you have traveled, the weather, the length of your stay.

Those to avoid include politics and religious beliefs.

Punctuality

Punctuality will be much appreciated.

Public manners

Gesture with your entire hand during conversation. Pointing with one or two fingers is considered rude.

Avoid showing the soles of your shoes.

Your feet should be used for walking—nothing else. Feet are considered unclean parts of the body and should never, for instance, be used for moving anything (i.e., a chair closer to a table).

Business entertaining

Expect all courses to be served simultaneously.

If you are invited to a person's home for dinner, flowers or a box of candy are considered appropriate gifts.

Avoid giving gifts when establishing a business relationship. The gesture could be perceived as a bribe.

When it is appropriate to give a gift, expect it to be refused a few times before it is accepted. Express your own gratitude once it has been accepted.

When doing business in South Korea

Greetings

When meeting someone, a slight bow is appropriate. When two people meet, the junior ranking person initiates the greeting to the senior ranking person.

When meeting a Korean woman, a man should wait for her to extend a handshake. A businesswoman from overseas should initiate a handshake with Korean men and women.

The term "son sae nim" means "respected person." It is used after either the family name or full name as a sign of respect. If you don't know a person's name, it is appropriate to use this title by itself.

While most cultures use two names, Koreans use three—a family name, a generational or clan name, and a given name. Family names tend to be one syllable long and clan names typically consist of two syllables.

It is considered good manners to acknowledge an older person by standing when the person enters a room.

One way to show respect for elders is by lowering your eyes.

Conversation

It is good manners to comment on the good health of an older person. Although compliments are much appreciated, it is considered polite for them to be denied.

Because Koreans place a high value on families, this is a good topic for discussion.

Topics to avoid include politics (especially any topic related to socialism and communism).

Avoid any type of disagreement in public.

Punctuality

Although Koreans do not put a particularly high value on punctuality, Westerners should nevertheless make an effort to be prompt.

Public manners

Loud laughter is considered rude. When laughing in public, cover your mouth.

Nose blowing is also considered to be in poor taste and should be done in private.

Be sure to remove your shoes before entering a temple or a person's home.

A hug or patting another on the back is considered rude.

Business entertaining

It is more common for entertaining to take place at a restaurant or bar (without spouses), rather than in a person's home.

If you are invited to a person's home, be sure to take a modest gift (such as flowers), offering the gift with both hands. Bear in mind that it is considered polite not to open a gift in front of the person giving it.

Expect all courses of a meal to be served at once.

Formal business professional attire is considered appropriate. Koreans believe that when you dress well, you acknowledge the importance of the occasion.

When doing business in the United Kingdom

Greetings

When meeting someone, respect space by maintaining a two arm's-length distance. If a person has an honorary title, it should be used in conversation—even among acquaintances. Use last names unless invited to do otherwise.

Men should wait for a British woman to extend her hand before shaking hands. When meeting someone, rather than saying, "It's nice to meet you," a more appropriate response is, "How do you do?"

Conversation

Refrain from asking the British, "What do you do?" This question is considered too personal.

When discussing individuals from the United Kingdom, (England, Scotland, Wales, and Northern Ireland) refer to them as the "British." Just to be on the safe side, avoid using the term "English" to describe anyone.

Avoid discussing politics and religion.

Punctuality

Promptness is appreciated.

Public manners

Your hands should always be visible. It is considered rude for hands to be in pockets. When pointing to something, do so with your head rather than with your fingers. Avoid wearing striped ties. (Why risk unintended mimicry of colors associated with British regiments?)

Don't make the victory sign with your palm facing inward. This is considered an obscene gesture in the U.K. Instead, make sure your palms face outward.

Business entertaining

If you are invited to someone's home and choose to take a gift, be sure it is a modest one. Gifts that cost more than $15 to $20 (U.S. currency) may embarrass the receiver.

Bibliography

Allen, Derek. *Addressing Overseas Business Letters*. St. Edmundsbury Press, 1988.

At Ease Inc., *Where Have All The Dress Rules Gone?* Video Series, 1997.

At Ease Inc., Business Etiquette Certification Program. Three-day session, 1995.

At Ease Inc., *Gaining The Competitive Edge Through Business Etiquette* Video Series, 1989.

Axtell, Roger, with Tami Briggs, Margaret Corcoran, and Mary Beth Lamb. *Do's and Taboos Around The World For Women in Business*. John Wiley & Sons, Inc., 1997.

Axtell, Roger. *Do's and Taboos Around the World*. Compiled by The Parker Pen Company. 3rd edition. John Wiley & Sons, Inc. 1993.

Axtell, Roger. *Do's and Taboos of Hosting International Visitors*. John Wiley & Sons, Inc., 1990.

Baldridge, Letitia. *Everyday Business Etiquette.* Barron's Educational Series, Inc., 1996.

Braganti, Nancy and Devine, Elizabeth. *The Travelers' Guide to European Customs & Manners.* Meadowbrook, Inc., 1984.

Brooks, Dr. Michael. *Instant Rapport.* Warner Books, Inc., 1989.

Brooks, Dr. Michael. *The Power of Business Rapport.* HarperCollins Publishers, 1991.

Budworth, Jeff. *Instant Recall.* Bob Adams, Inc., 1991.

Communication Briefings, *The 76 Most-Common Grammar Errors.* Communication Publications & Resources, 1992.

Gabor, Don. *Speaking Your Mind in 101 Difficult Situations.* Fireside Books, Simon & Schuster, 1994.

Kenna, Peggy and Lacy, Sondra. *Business China.* Passport Books, NTC Publishing, 1994.

Kenna, Peggy and Lacy, Sondra. *Business France.* Passport Books, NTC Publishing, 1994.

Kenna, Peggy and Lacy, Sondra. *Business Mexico.* Passport Books, NTC Publishing, 1994.

Kenna, Peggy and Lacy, Sondra. *Business Taiwan.* Passport Books, NTC Publishing, 1994.

Jessup, Jay and Maggie. *Doing Business in Mexico.* Prima Publishing, 1993.

Kaumeyer, Jr., Richard. *How To Write And Speak In Business.* Van Nostrand Reinhold Company Inc., 1985.

Leeds, Dorothy. *Smart Questions.* McGraw-Hill, 1987.

Ling, Mona. *How to Increase Sales and Put Yourself Across by Telephone.* Prentice-Hall, Inc., 1963.

Martin, Judith. *Miss Manners' Audio Guide for the Turn of the Millennium.* St. Martin's Press, 1989.

Martin, Phyllis. *Word Watchers Handbook.* 3rd edition. St. Martin's Press, 1991.

Mole, John. *Mind Your Manners.* New Edition. Nicholas Brealey Publishing Limited, 1992.

Molloy, John. *New Women's Dress for Success.* Warner Books, Inc., 1996.

Morrison, Terri with Wayne A. Conway and George A. Borden, Ph.D. *Kiss, Bow, or Shake Hands.* Adams Media Corporation, 1994.

Post, Elizabeth. *Business Etiquette.* Harper & Row, 1990.

RoAne, Susan. *The Secrets of Savvy Networking*. Warner Books, Inc., 1993.

Roger, John and McWilliams, Peter. *Life 101*. Prelude Press, 1990.

Sabath, Ann Marie. *Business Etiquette In Brief*. Bob Adams Inc., 1993.

Sokolosky, Valerie. *The Little Instruction Book of Business Etiquette*. Honor Books, 1996.

Stewart, Marjabelle. *New Etiquette*. St. Martins Press, 1997.

Taylor, Emerson. *Graduates' Guide To Business Success*. Biography for Everyone, 1997.

Thomsett, Michael. *The Little Black Book of Business Etiquette*. AMACOM, a Division of American Management Association, 1991.

Weber, Mark and The Van Heusen Creative Design Group. *Dress Casually for Success... For Men*. McGraw Hill, 1997.

About the Author

Ann Marie Sabath is the founder of At Ease Inc., a Cincinnati-based company specializing in business protocol and etiquette programs. Over the past eight years, Ms. Sabath has served as the Business Manners Columnist for *The Washington Times*, *The Dayton Daily News*, *The Cincinnati Enquirer*, *The Dallas Times Herald,* and *Sales And Marketing Management Magazine*. Presently, she is the Business Manners Columnist for *Communication Briefings* and *The Cincinnati Downtowner*. Her book *Business Etiquette In Brief* was released in bookstores around the country in the spring of 1993. Her Business Etiquette Tips aired on CNBC's *Management Today* in the Spring of 1995, and her domestic and international training programs were the subject of features in *USA Today* and Delta Airlines' *Sky Magazine*. She has appeared twice on *Oprah!* as an expert on manners and etiquette.

Ms. Sabath and her staff have trained more than 20,000 people on how to use etiquette to gain the competitive edge. She has worked with such organizations as Procter & Gamble, Cap Gemini America, United Brands, the Huffy Corporation, Showtime Network Inc., Saks Fifth Avenue, SmithKline Beecham, BP America, Paychex, MCI, Marriott Corporation, and Salomon Brothers.

Index